ATTA TROLL

LECTOR HOUSE PUBLIC DOMAIN WORKS

ATTA TROLL

HEINRICH HEINE,
HERMAN SCHEFFAUER,
OSCAR LEVY

ISBN: 978-93-5344-855-4

Published: 1913

ATTA TROLL

FROM THE GERMAN OF
HEINRICH HEINE

BY

HERMAN SCHEFFAUER

WITH AN INTRODUCTION BY
DR OSCAR LEVY

AND SOME PEN AND INK SKETCHES BY
WILLY POGANY

1913

CONTENTS

INTRODUCTION

AN INTERPRETATION OF HEINRICH HEINE'S "ATTA TROLL"

THE who has visited the idyllic isle of Corfu must have seen, gleaming white amidst its surroundings of dark green under a sky of the deepest blue, the Greek villa which was erected there by Elizabeth, Empress of Austria. It is called the Achilleion. In its garden there is a small classic temple in which the Empress caused to be placed a marble statue of her most beloved of poets, Heinrich Heine. The statue represented the poet seated, his head bowed in profound melancholy, his cheeks thin and drawn and bearded, as in his last illness.

Elizabeth, Empress of Austria, felt a sentimental affinity with the poet; his unhappiness, his **Weltschmerz**, touched a responsive chord in her own unhappy heart. Intellectual sympathy with Heine's thought or tendencies there could have been little, for no woman has ever quite understood Heinrich Heine, who is still a riddle to most of the men of this age.

After the assassination of the hapless Empress, the beautiful villa was bought by the German Emperor. He at once ordered Heine's statue to be removed—whither no one knows. Royal (as well as popular) spite has before this been vented on dead or inanimate things—one need only ask Englishmen to remember what happened to the body of Oliver Cromwell. The Kaiser's action, by the way, did not pass unchallenged. Not only in Germany but in several other countries indignant voices were raised at the time, protesting against an act so insulting to the memory of the great singer, upholding the fame of Heine as a poet and denouncing the new master of the Achilleion for his narrow and prejudiced views on art and literature.

There was, however, a sound reason for the Imperial interference. Heinrich Heine was in his day an outspoken enemy of Prussia, a severe critic of the House of Hohenzollern and of other Royal houses of Germany. He was one who held in scorn the principles of State and government that are honoured in Germany, and elsewhere, to this very day. He was one of those poets—of whom the nineteenth century produced only a few, but those amongst the greatest—who had begun to distrust the capacity of the reigning aristocracy, who knew what to expect from the rising bourgeoisie, and who were nevertheless not romantic enough to believe in the people and the wonderful possibilities hidden in them. These poets—one and all—have taken up a very negative attitude towards their contemporaries and have given voice to their anger and disappointment over the pettiness of the society and government of their time in words full of satire and contempt.

Of course, the echo on the part of their audiences has not been wanting. All these po-

ets have experienced a fate surprisingly similar, and their relationship to their respective countries reminds one of those unhappy matrimonial alliances which—for social or religious reasons—no divorce can ever dissolve. And, worse than that, no separation either, for a poet is—through his mother tongue—so intimately wedded to his country that not even a separation can effect any sort of relief in such a desperate case. All of them have tried separation, all of them have lived in estrangement from their country—we might almost say that only the local and lesser poets of the last century have stayed at home—and yet in spite of this separation the mutual recriminations of these passionate poetical husbands and their obstinate national wives have never ceased. Again and again we hear the male partner making proposals to win his spouse to better and nobler ways, again and again he tries to "educate her up to himself" and endeavours to direct her anew, pointing out to her the danger of her unruly and stupid behaviour; again and again his loving approaches are thwarted by the well-known waywardness of the feminine character, and so all his friendly admonitions habitually turn into torrents of abuse and vilification. There have been many unhappy unions in the world, but the compulsory mésalliances of such great nineteenth-century writers as Heine, Byron, Stendhal, Gobineau, and Nietzsche with Mesdames Britannia, Gallia, and Germania, those otherwise highly respectable ladies, easily surpass in grotesqueness anything that has come to us through divorce court proceedings in England and America. That, as every one will agree, is saying a good deal.

The German Emperor, as I have said, had some justification for his action, some motives that do credit, if not to his intellect, at least to what in our days best takes the place of intellect; that is to say his character and his principles of government. The German Emperor appears at least to realize how offensive and, from his point of view, dangerous, the spirit of Heinrich Heine is to this very day, how deeply his satire cuts into questions of religion and State, how impatient he is of everything which the German Emperor esteems and venerates in his innermost heart. But the German people, on the whole, and certainly all foreigners, have long ago forgiven the poet, not because they have understood the dead bard better than the Emperor, but because they understood him less well. It is always easier to forgive an offender if you do not understand him too well, it is likewise easier to forgive him if your memory be short. And the peoples likewise resemble our womenfolk in this respect, that as soon as they are widowed of their poets, they easily forget all the unpleasantness that had ever existed between them and their dead husbands. It is then and only then that they discover the good qualities of their dead consorts and go about telling everybody "what a wonderful man he was." Their behaviour reminds me of a picture I once saw in a French comic paper. It represented a widow who, in order to hear her deceased husband's voice, had a gramophone put at his empty place at the breakfast table. And every morning she sat opposite that gramophone weeping quietly into her handkerchief, gazing mournfully at the instrument—decorated with her dead hubby's tasselled cap—and listening to the voice of the dear departed. But the only words which came out of the gramophone every morning were: Mais fiche-moi donc la paix—tu m'empêches de lire mon journal! *(For goodness' sake, leave me alone and let me read my paper.) This, however, did not appear to disturb the sentimental widow at all, as little indeed as a good sentimental people resents being abused by its dead poet.*

And how our poet did abuse them during his life! And not only during his life, for Heine would not have been a great poet if his loves and hatreds, his censure and his praise had not outlasted his life, nay, had not come to real life only after his death. Thus the shafts of wit and satire which Heine levelled at his age and his country will seem singularly modern to the reader of to-day. It is this peculiar modern significance and application that has been one of the two reasons for presenting to the English public the first popular edition of Heine's lyrico-satiric masterpiece "Atta Troll." The other reason is the fine quality of the translation, made by one who is himself well known as a poet, my friend Herman Scheffauer. I venture to say that it renders in a remarkable degree the elusive brilliance, wit, and tenderness of the German original.

The poem begins in a sprightly fashion full of airy mockery and romantic lyricism. The reader is beguiled as with music and led on as in a dance. Heine himself called it das letzte freie Waldlied der Romantik ("The last free woodland-song of Romanticism"); and so we hear the alluring sound of flutes and harps, we listen to the bells ringing from lonely chapels in the forest, and many beautiful flowers nod to us, the mysterious blue flower amongst them. Then our eyes rejoice at the sight of fair maidens, whose nude and slender bodies gleam from under their floods of golden hair, who ride on white horses and throw us provocative glances, that warm and quicken our innermost hearts. But just as we are on the point of responding to their fond entreaties we are startled by the cracking of the wild hunter's whip, and we hear the loud hallo and huzza of his band, and see them galloping across our path in the eerie mysterious moonlight. Yes, in "Atta Troll" there is plenty of that moonshine, of that tender sentimentality, which used to be the principal stock-in-trade of the German Romanticist.

But this moonshine and all the other paraphernalia of the Romantic School Heine handled with all the greater skill, inasmuch as he was no longer a real Romanticist when he wrote "Atta Troll." He had left the Romantic School long ago, not without (as he himself tells us) "having given a good thrashing to his schoolmaster." He was now a Greek, a follower of Spinoza and Goethe. He was a Romantique défroqué—one who had risen above his neurotic fellow-poets and their hazy ideas and wild endeavours. But for this very reason he is able to use their mode of expression with so much the greater skill, and, knowing all their shortcomings, he could give to his Dreamland a semblance of reality which they could never achieve. Only after having left a town are we in a position to judge the height of its church steeple, only as exiles do we begin to see the right relation in which our country stands to the rest of the world, and only a poet who had bidden farewell to his party and school, who had freed himself from Romanticism, could give us the last, the truest, the most beautiful poem of Romanticism.

It is possible, even probable, that "Atta Troll" will appeal to a majority of readers, not through its satire, but through its wonderful lyrical and romantic qualities—our age being inclined to look askance at satire, at least at true satire, at satire that, as the current phrase goes, "means business." Weak satire, aimless satire, humour, caricature—that is to say satire which uses blank cartridges—this age of ours will readily endure, nay heartily welcome; but of true satire, of satire that goes in for powder and shot, that does not only crack, but kill, it is mortally, and, if one comes to think of it rightly, afraid. But let even those who object to powder and shot approach "Atta Troll" without fear or misgiving. They will not be disappointed. They will find in this work proof of the old truth that a satirist is always and originally a man of high ideals and imagination. They will gain an insight into his much slandered soul, which is always that of a great poet. They will readily understand that this *poet only became a satirist through the vivacity of his imagination, through the strength of his poetic vision, through his optimistic belief in humanity and its possibilities; and that it was precisely this great faith which forced him to become a satirist, because he could not endure to see all his pure ideals and the possibilities of perfection soiled and trampled upon by thoughtless mechanics, aimless mockers and babbling reformers. The humorist may be—and very often is—a sceptic, a pessimist, a nihilist; the satirist is invariably a believer, an optimist, an idealist. For let this dangerous man only come face to face, not with his enemies, but with his ideals, and you will see—as in "Atta Troll"—what a generous friend, what an ardent lover, what a great poet he is. Thus no one will be in the least disturbed by Heine's satire: on the contrary, those who object to it on principle will hardly be aware of it, so delighted will they be with the wonderful imagination, the glowing descriptions, and the passionate lyrics in which the poetry of "Atta Troll" abounds. The poem may be and will be read by them as "Gulliver's Travels" is read to-day by young and old, by poet and politician alike, not for its original satire, but for its picturesque, dramatic, and enthralling tale.*

But let those who still believe that writing is fighting, and not sham-fighting only, those who hold that a poet is a soldier of the pen and therefore the most dangerous of all soldiers, those who feel that our age needs a hailstorm of satire, let these, I say, look closer at the wonderfully ideal figures that pass before them in the pale mysterious light. Let them listen more intently to the flutes and harps and they will discover quite a different melody beneath—a melody by no means bewitching or soothing, nor inviting us to dreams, sweet forgetfulness, soft couches, and tender embraces, but a shrill and mocking tune that is at times insolently discordant and that strikes us as decidedly modern, realistic, and threatening. As the poet himself expressed it in his dedication to Varnhagen von Ense:

> *"Aye, my friend, such strains arise*
> *From the dream-time that is dead*
> Though some modern trills may oft
> Caper through the ancient theme.
>
> *"Spite of waywardness thou'lt find*
> Here and there a note of pain...."

Let their ears seek to catch these painful notes. Let their eyes accustom themselves to the deceitful light of the moon; let them endeavour to pierce through the romanticism on the surface to the underlying meaning of the poem.... A little patience and we shall see clearly....

Atta Troll, the dancing bear, is the representative of the people. He has—by means of the French Revolution, of course—broken his fetters and escaped to the freedom of the mountains. Here he indulges in that familiar ranting of a sansculotte, *his heart and mouth brimming over with what Heine calls* frecher Gleichheitsschwindel *("the barefaced swindle of equality"). His hatred is above all directed against the masters from whose bondage he has just escaped, that is to say against all mankind as a race. As a "true and noble bear" he simply detests these human beings with their superior airs and impudent smiles, those arrogant wretches, who fancy themselves something lofty, because they eat cooked meat and know a few tricks and sciences. Animals, if properly trained, if only equality of opportunity were given to them, could learn these tricks just as well—there is therefore no earthly reason why*

"these men,
Cursèd arch-aristocrats,
Should with haughty insolence
Look upon the world of beasts."

The beasts, so Atta Troll declares, ought not to allow themselves to be treated in this wise. They ought to combine amongst themselves, for it is only by means of proper union that the requisite degree of strength can ever be attained. After the establishment of this powerful union they should try to enforce their programme and demand the abolition of private property and of human privileges:

"And its first great law shall be
For God's creatures one and all
Equal rights — no matter what
Be their faith, or hide, or smell,

"Strict equality! Each ass
May become Prime Minister,
On the other hand the lion
Shall bear corn unto the mill."

This outrageous diatribe of the freed slave cuts deeply into the poet's heart. He, the poet, does not believe in equal, but in the "holy inborn" rights of men, the rights of valid birth, the rights of the man of ἀρετή. He, the poet, the admirer of Napoleon, believes in the latter's la carrière ouverte aux talents, *but not in opportunity given to every dunce or dancing bear. He holds Atta Troll's opinion to be "high treason against the majesty of humanity," and since he can endure this no longer, he sets out one fine morning to hunt the insolent bear in his mountain fastnesses.*

A strange being, however, accompanies him. This is a man of the name of Lascaro, a somewhat abnormal fellow, who is very thin, very pale, and apparently in very poor health. He is consequently not exactly a pleasant comrade for the chase: he does not seem to enjoy the sport at all, and his one endeavour is to get through with his task without losing more of his strength and health. Even now he is more of an automaton than a human being, more dead than alive, and yet — greatest of all miseries! — he is not allowed to die. For he has a mother, the witch Uraka, who keeps him artificially alive by anointing him every night with magic salve and giving him such diabolic advice as will be useful to him during the day. By means of the sham health she gives to her son, the magic bullets she casts for him, the tricks and wiles she teaches him, Lascaro is enabled to find the track of Atta Troll, to lure him out of his lair and to lay him low with a treacherous shot.

Who is this silent Lascaro and his mysterious mother, whom the poet seems to hold in as slight regard as the noisy Atta Troll? Who is this Lascaro, whose methods he deprecates, whose health he doubts, whose cold ways and icy smiles make him shudder? Who is this chilliest of all monsters? The chilliest of all monsters — we may find the answer in "Zarathustra" — is the State: and our Lascaro is nothing else than the spirit of reactionary government, kept artificially alive by his old witch-mother, the spirit of Feudalism. The nightly anointing of Lascaro is a parody on the revival of mediæval customs, by means of which the frightened aristocracy of Europe in the middle of the last century tried to stem the tide of the French Revolution — the anointed of the Lord becoming in Heine's poem the *anointed of the witch. But in spite of his nightly massage, our Lascaro does not gain much strength or spirit: no mediæval salves, no feudal pills, no witch's spell, will ever cure him. Not even a wizard's experiments (we may add, with that greater insight bestowed upon us by history) could do him any good, not even the astute magic tricks that were lavished upon the patient in Heine's time by that arch wizard, the Austrian Minister Metternich. For we must not forget the time in which "Atta Troll" was written, the time of the omnipotent Metternich! Let us recall to our memories this cool, clever, callous statesman, who founded and set the Holy Alliance against the Revolution, who calmly shot down the German Atta Troll, who skilfully strangled and stifled that promising poetical school, "Young Germany," to which Heine belonged. Let us recall this man, who likewise artificially revived the old religion and the old feudalism, who repolished and regilded the scutcheons of the decadent aristocracy, and who, despite all his energy, had at heart no belief in his work, no joy in his task, no faith in the anointed dummies he brought to life again in Europe—and those puzzling personalities of Uraka and Lascaro will be elucidated to us by a real historical example.*

Metternich is now part of history. But, alas! we cannot likewise banish into that limbo of the past those two superfluous individuals, the revolutionary Atta Troll and the reactionary Lascaro. Alas! we cannot join the joyful, but inwardly so hopeless, band of those who sing the pæan of eternal progress, who pretend to believe that the times are always "changing for the better." Let these good people open their eyes, and they will see that Atta Troll was not shot down in the valley of Roncesvalles, but that he is still alive, very much alive, and making a dreadful noise, and that not in the Pyrenees, but just outside our doors, where he still keeps haranguing about equality and liberty and occasionally breaks his fetters and escapes from his masters. And when this occurs, then that icy monster Lascaro is likewise seen, with his hard, pallid face and his joyless mouth, and his disgust with his own task and his doubts and disbeliefs in himself. He still carries his gun and he still possesses some of that craftiness which his mother the witch has taught him, and he still knows how to entrap that poor, stupid Atta Troll, and to shoot him down when the spirit of "order and government," the spirit of a soulless capitalism, requires it.

No, there is very little feeling in the man as yet, and he seems as difficult to move as ever. There is apparently only one thing that can rouse him into action, and that is when a poet appears, one who knows the truth and who dares to speak the truth not only about Atta Troll, the people, but also about its Lascaros, its leaders, its emperors, and kings. Then and then only his hard features change, and his affected self-possession leaves him, then and then only his mask of calmness is thrown off, and he waxes very angry with the poet, and has his name banished from his court and his statues turned out of his cities and villas—nay, he would even level his gun to slay the truth-telling poet as he slew Atta Troll.

From which we may see that the modern Lascaro has become a sort of Don Quixote—for, truly is it not the height of folly for a mortal emperor to shoot at an immortal poet?

OSCAR LEVY

London, 1913

PREFACE BY HEINE

"ATTA TROLL" was composed in the late autumn of 1841, and appeared as a fragment in The Elegant World, of which my friend Laube had at that time resumed the editorship. The shape and contents of the poem were forced to conform to the narrow necessities of that periodical. I wrote at first only those cantos which might be printed and even these suffered many variations. It was my intention to issue the work later in its full completeness, but this commendable resolve remained unfulfilled—like all the mighty works of the Germans—such as the cathedral of Cologne, the God of Schelling, the Prussian Constitution, and the like. This also happened to "Atta Troll"—he was never finished. In such imperfect form, indifferently bolstered up and rounded only from without, do I now set him before the public, obedient to an impulse which certainly does not proceed from within.

"Atta Troll," as I have said, originated in the late autumn of 1841, at the time when the great mob which my enemies of various complexions, had drummed together against me, had not quite ceased its noise. It was a very large mob and indeed I would never have believed that Germany could produce so many rotten apples as then flew about my head! Our Fatherland is a blessed country! Citrons and oranges certainly do not grow here, and the laurel ekes out but a miserable existence, but rotten apples thrive in the happiest abundance, and never a great poet of ours but could write feelingly of them! On the occasion of that hue and cry in which I was to lose both my head and my laurels it happened that I lost neither. All the absurd accusations which were used to incite the mob against me have since then been miserably annihilated, even without my condescending to refute them. Time justified me, and the various German States have even, as I must most gratefully acknowledge, done me good service in this respect. The warrants of arrest which at every German station past the frontier await the return of this poet, are thoroughly renovated every year during the holy Christmastide, when the little candles glow merrily on the Christmas trees. It is this insecurity of the roads which has almost destroyed my pleasure in travelling through the German meads. I am therefore celebrating my Christmas in an alien land, and it will be as an exile in a foreign country that I shall end my days.

But those valiant champions of Light and Truth who accuse me of fickleness and servility, are able to go about quite securely in the Fatherland—as well-stalled servants of the State, as dignitaries of a Guild, or as regular guests of a club where of evenings they may regale themselves with the vinous juices of Father Rhine and with "sea-surrounded Schleswig-Holstein" oysters.

It was my express intention to indicate in the foregoing at what period "Atta Troll" was written. At that time the so-called art of political poetry was in full flower. The opposition, as Ruge says, sold its leather and became poetry. The Muses were given strict orders that they were thenceforth no longer to gad about in a wanton, easy-going fashion, but *would be compelled to enter into national service, possibly as* vivandières *of liberty or as washerwomen of Christian-Germanic nationalism. Especially were the bowers of the German bards afflicted by that vague and sterile pathos, that useless fever of enthusiasm which, with absolute disregard for death, plunges itself into an ocean of generalities. This always reminds me of the American sailor who was so madly enthusiastic over General Jackson that he sprang from the mast-head into the sea, crying out: "I die for General Jackson!" Yes, even though we Germans as yet possessed no fleet, still we had plenty of sailors who were willing to die for General Jackson, in prose or verse. In those days talent was a rather questionable gift, for it brought one under suspicion of being a loose character. After thousands of years of grubbing deliberation, Impotence, sick and limping Impotence, at last discovered its greatest weapon against the over-encouragement of genius — it discovered, in fact, the antithesis between Talent and Character. It was almost personally flattering to the great masses when they heard it said that good, average people were certainly poor musicians as a rule, but that, on the other hand, fine musicians were not usually good people — that goodness was the important thing in this world and not music. Empty-Head now beat resolutely upon his full Heart, and Sentiment was trumps. I recall an author of that day who accounted his inability to write as a peculiar merit in himself, and who, because of his wooden style, was given a silver cup of honour.*

By the eternal gods! at that time it became necessary to defend the inalienable rights of the spirit, above all in poetry. Inasmuch as I have made this defence the chief business of my life, I have kept it constantly before me in this poem whose tone and theme are both a protest against the plebiscite of the tribunes of the times. And verily, even the first fragments of "Atta Troll" which saw the light, aroused the wrath of my heroic worthies, my dear Romans, who accused me not only of a literary but also of a social reaction, and even of mocking the loftiest human ideals. As to the esthetic worth of my poem — of that I thought but little, as I still do to-day — I wrote it solely for my own joy and pleasure, in the fanciful dreamy manner of that romantic school in which I whiled away my happiest years of youth, and then wound up by thrashing the schoolmaster. Possibly in this regard my poem is to be condemned. But thou liest, Brutus, thou too, Cassius, and even thou, Asinius, when ye declare that my mockery is levelled against those ideals which constitute the noble achievements of man, for which I too have wrought and suffered so much. No, it is just because the poet constantly sees these ideas before him in all their clarity and greatness that he is forced into irresistible laughter when he beholds how raw, awkward, and clumsy these ideas may appear when interpreted by a narrow circle of contemporary spirits. Then perforce must he jest about their thick temporal hides — bear hides. There are mirrors which are ground in so irregular a way that even an Apollo would behold himself as a caricature in them, and invite laughter. But we do not laugh at the god but merely at his distorted image.

Another word. Need I lay any special emphasis upon the fact that the parodying of one of Freiligrath's poems, which here and there somewhat saucily titters from the lines of "Atta Troll," in no wise constitutes a disparagement of that poet? I value him highly, especially at present, and account him one of the most important poets who have arisen in Germany since the Revolution of 1830. His first collection of poems came to my notice rather late, namely just at the time when I was composing "Atta Troll." The fact that the Moorish Prince affected me so comically was no doubt due to my particular mood at that time. Moreover, this work of his is usually vaunted as his best. To such readers as may not be acquainted with this production—and I doubt not such may be found in China and Ja-pan, and even along the banks of the Niger and Senegal—I would call attention to the fact that the Blackamoor King, who at the beginning of the poem steps from his white tent like an eclipsed moon, is beloved by a black beauty over whose dusky features nod white ostrich plumes. But, eager for war, he leaves her, and enters into the battles of the blacks, "where rattles the drum decorated with skulls," but, alas! here he finds his black Waterloo, and is sold by the victors unto the whites. They take the noble African to Europe and here we find him in a company of itinerant circus folk who intrust him with the care of the Turkish drum at their performances. There he stands, dark and solemn, at the entrance to the ring, and drums. But as he drums he thinks of his erstwhile greatness, remembers, too, that he was once an absolute monarch on the far, far banks of the Niger, that he hunted lions and tigers:

> *"His eye grew moist; with hollow thunder*
> *He beat the drum, till it sprang in sunder."*

HEINRICH HEINE

Written at Paris, 1846

ATTA TROLL

Out of the gleaming, shimmering tents of white
Steps the Prince of the Moors in his armour bright—
So out of the slumbering clouds of night,
The moon in its dark eclipse takes flight.

"The Prince of Blackamoors,"
by Ferdinand Freiligrath.

CANTO I

Ringed about by mountains dark,
Rising peak on sullen peak,
And by furious waterfalls
Lulled to slumber, like a dream

White within the valley lies
Cauterets. Each villa neat
Sports a balcony whereon
Lovely ladies stand and laugh.

Heartily they laugh and look
Down upon the crowded square
Where unto a bag-pipe's drone
He- and she-bear strut and dance.

Atta Troll is dancing there
With his Mumma, dusky mate,
While in wonderment the Basques
Shout aloud and clap their hands.

Stiff with pride and gravity
Dances noble Atta Troll,
Though his shaggy partner knows
Neither dignity nor shame.

I am even fain to think
She is verging on the can-can,
For her shameless wagging hints
Of the gay *Grande Chaumière*

Even he, the showman brave,
Holding her with loosened chain,
Marks the immorality
Of her most immodest dance.

So at times he lays the lash
Straight across her inky back,
Till the mountains wake and shout
Echoes to her frenzied howls.

On the showman's pointed hat
Six Madonnas made of lead
Shield him from the foeman's balls
Or invasions of the louse.

And a gaudy altar-cloth
From his shoulders hanging down,
Makes a proper sort of cloak,
Hiding pistol and a knife.

In his youth a monk was he,
Then became a robber chief;
Later, in Don Carlos' ranks,
He combined the other two.

When Don Carlos, forced to flee,
Bade his Table Round farewell,
All his Paladins resolved
Straight to learn an honest trade.

Herr Schnapphahnski turned a scribe,
And our staunch Crusader here
Just a showman, with his bears
Trudging up and down the land.

And in every market-place
For the people's pence they dance—
In the square at Cauterets
Atta Troll is dancing now!

Atta Troll, the Forest King,
He who ruled on mountain-heights,
Now to please the village mob,
Dances in his doleful chains.

Worse and worse! for money vile
He must dance who, clad in might,
Once in majesty of terror
Held the world a sorry thing!

When the memories of his youth
And his lost dominions green,
Smite the soul of Atta Troll,
Mournful sobs escape his breast.

And he scowls as scowled the black
Monarch famed of Freiligrath;
In his rage he dances badly,
As the darkey badly drummed.

Yet compassion none he wins,—
Only laughter! Juliet
From her balcony is laughing

At his wild, despairing bounds.

Juliet, you see, is French,
And was born without a soul—
Lives for mere externals—but
Her externals are so fair!

Like a net of tender gleams
Are the glances of her eye,
And our hearts like little fishes,
Fall and struggle in that net.

CANTO II

When the dusky Moorish Prince
Sung by poet Freiligrath
Beat upon his mighty drum
Till the drumskin crashed and broke—

Thrilling must that crash have been—
Likewise hard upon the ear—
But just fancy when a bear
Breaks away from captive chains!

Swift the laughter and the pipes
Cease. What yells of fear arise!
From the square the people rush
And the gentle dames grow pale.

Yea, from all his slavish bonds
Atta Troll has torn him free.
Suddenly! With mighty leaps
Through the narrow streets he runs.

Room enough is his, I trow!
Up the jagged cliffs he climbs,
Flings down one contemptuous look,
Then is lost within the hills.

Lone within the market-place
Mumma and her master stand—
Raging, now he grasps his hat,
Cursing, casts it on the earth,

Tramples on it, kicks and flouts
The Madonnas, tears the cloak
Off his foul and naked back,
Yells and blasphemes horribly

'Gainst the base ingratitude
Of the race of sable bears.
Had he not been kind to Troll?
Taught him dancing free of charge?

Everything this monster owed him,
Even life. For some had bid,
All in vain! three hundred marks
For the hide of Atta Troll.

Like some carven form of grief
There the poor black Mumma stands
On her hind feet, with her paws
Pleading with the raging clown.

But on her the raging clown
Looses now his twofold wrath;
Beats her; calls her Queen Christine,
Dame Muñoz—Putana too....

All this happened on a fair
Sunny summer afternoon.
And the night which followed, ah!
Was superb and wonderful.

Of that night a part I spent
On a small white balcony;
Juliet was at my side
And we viewed the passing stars.

"Fairer far," she sighed, "the stars
Which in Paris I have seen,
When upon a winter's night
In the muddy streets they shine."

CANTO III

Dream of summer nights! How vain
Is my fond fantastic song.
Quite as vain as Love and Life,
And Creator and Creation.

Subject to his own sweet will,
Now in gallop, now in flight,
So my Pegasus, my darling,
Revels through the realms of myth.

Ah, no plodding cart-horse he!
Harnessed up for citizens,
Nor a ramping party-hack
Full of showy kicks and neighs.

For my little wingèd steed's
Hoofs are shod with solid gold
And his bridle, dragging free,
Is a rope of gleaming pearls.

Bear me wheresoe'er thou wouldst—
To some lofty mountain-trail
Where the torrents toss and shriek
Warnings over folly's gulf.

Bear me through the silent vales
Where the solemn oaks arise
From whose twisted roots there well
Ancient springs of fairy lore.

There, oh, let me drink—mine eyes
Let me lave—Oh, how I thirst
For that flashing wonder-spring,
Full of wisdom and of light.

All my blindness flees. My glance
Pierces to the dimmest cave,
To the lair of Atta Troll,
And his speech I understand!

Strange it is—this bearish speech
Hath a most familiar ring!
Once, methinks, I heard such tones
In my own dear native land.

CANTO IV

Roncesvalles, thou noble vale!
When thy golden name I hear,
Then the lost blue flower blooms
Once again within my heart!

All the glittering world of dreams
Rises from its hoary gulf,
And with great and ghostly eyes
Stares upon me till I quake!

What a stir and clang! The Franks
Battle with the Saracens,
While a thin, despairing wail
Pours like blood from Roland's horn.

In the Vale of Roncesvalles,
Close beside great Roland's Gap—
So 'twas named because the Knight
Once to clear himself a path.

Now this youngest was the pet
Of his mother. Once in play
Chewing off his tiny ear—
She devoured it for love.

A most genial youth is he,
Clever in gymnastic tricks,
Throwing somersaults as clever
As dear Massmann's somersaults.

Blossom of the pristine cult,
For the mother-tongue he raves,
Scorning all the senseless jargon
Of the Romans and the Greeks.

"Fresh and pious, gay and free,"
Hating all that smacks of soap
Or the modern craze for baths—

Verily like Massmann too!

Most inspired is this youth
When he clambers up the tree
Which from out the hollow gorge
Rears itself along the cliff,

Rears and lifts unto the crest
Where at night this jolly band
Squat and loll about their sire
In the twilight dim and cool.

Gladly there the father bear
Tells them stories of the world,
Of strange cities and their folk,
And of all he suffered too,

Suffered like Ulysses great—
Differing slightly from this brave
Since his black Penelope
Never parted from his side.

Loudly too prates Atta Troll
Of the mighty meed of praise
Which by practice of his art
He had wrung from humankind.

Young and old, so runs his tale,
Cheered in wonder and in joy,
When in market-squares he danced
To the bag-pipe's pleasant skirl.

And the ladies most of all—
Ah, what gentle connoisseurs!—
Rendered him their mad applause
And full many a tender glance.

Artists' vanity! Alas,
Pensively the dancing-bear
Thinks upon those happy hours
When his talents pleased the crowd.

Seized with rapture self-inspired,
He would prove his words by deeds,
Prove himself no boaster vain
But a master in the art.

Swiftly from the ground he springs,
Stands on hinder paws erect,
Dances then his favourite dance
As of old—the great Gavotte.

Dumb, with open jaws the cubs

Gaze upon their father there
As he makes his wondrous leaps
In the moonshine to and fro.

CANTO V

In his cavern by his young,
Atta Troll in moody wise
Lies upon his back and sucks
Fiercely at his paws, and growls:

"Mumma, Mumma, dusky pearl
That from out the sea of life
I had gathered, in that sea
I have lost thee once again!

"Shall I never see thee more?
Shall it be beyond the grave
Where from earthly travail free
Thy bright spirit spreads its wings?

"Ah, if I might once again
Lick my darling Mumma's snout—
Lovely snout as dear to me
As if smeared with honey-dew.

"Might I only sniff once more
That aroma sweet and rare
Of my dear and dusky mate—
Scent as sweet as roses' breath!

"But, alas! my Mumma lies
In the bondage of that tribe
Which believes itself Creation's
Lords and bears the name of Man!

"Death! Damnation! that these men—
Cursèd arch-aristocrats!
Should with haughty insolence
Look upon the world of beasts!

"They who steal our wives and young,
Chain us, beat us, slaughter us!—
Yea, they slaughter us and trade
In our corpses and our pelts!

"More, they deem these hideous deeds
Justified — particularly
Towards the noble race of bears —
This they call the Rights of Man!

"Rights of Man? The Rights of Man!
Who bestowed these rights on you?
Surely 'twas not Mother Nature —
She is ne'er unnatural!

"Rights of Man! Who gave to you
All these privileges rare?
Verily it was not Reason —
Ne'er unreasonable she!

"Is it, men, because you roast,
Stew or fry or boil your meat,
Whilst our own is eaten raw,
That you deem yourselves so grand?

"In the end 'tis all the same.
Food alone can ne'er impart
Any worth; — none noble is
Save who nobly acts and feels!

"Are you better, human things,
Just because success attends
All your arts and sciences?
No mere wooden-heads are we!

"Are there not most learnèd dogs!
Horses, too, that calculate
Quite as well as bankers? — Hares
Who have skill in beating drums?

"Are not beavers most adroit
In the craft of waterworks?
Were not clyster-pipes invented
Through the cleverness of storks?

"Do not asses write critiques?
Do not apes play comedy?
Could there be a greater actress
Than Batavia the ape?

"Do the nightingales not sing?
Is not Freiligrath a bard?
Who e'er sang the lion's praise
Better than his brother mule?

"In the art of dance have I
Gone as far as Raumer quite
In the art of letters — can he

Scribble better than I dance?

"Why should mortal men be placed
O'er us animals? Though high
You may lift your heads, yet low
In those heads your thoughts do crawl.

"Human wights, why better, pray,
Than ourselves? Is it because
Smooth and slippery is your skin?
Snakes have that advantage too!

"Human hordes! two-legged snakes!
Well indeed I understand
That those flapping pantaloons
Must conceal your serpent hides!

"Children, Oh, beware of these
Vile and hairless miscreants!
O my daughters, never trust
Monsters that wear pantaloons!"

But no further will I tell
How this bear with arrogant
Fallacies of equal rights
Raved against the human race

For I too am man, and never
As a man will I repeat
All this vile disparagement,
Bound to give most grave offence.

Yes, I too am man, am placed
O'er the other mammals all!
Shall I sell my birthright? — No!
Nor my interest betray.

Ever faithful unto man,
I will fight all other beasts.
I will battle for the high
Holy inborn rights of man!

CANTO VI

Yet for man who forms the higher
Class of animals 'twere well
That betimes he should discover
What the lower thinks of him.

Verily within those drear
Strata of the world of brutes,
In those lower social layers
There is misery, pride and wrath.

Laws which Nature hath decreed,
Customs sanctioned long by Time,
And for centuries established,
They deny with pertest tongue.

Grumbling, there the old instil
Evil doctrines in the young,
Doctrines which endanger all
Human culture on the Earth.

"Children!" grunts our Atta Troll,
As he tosses to and fro
On his hard and stony couch,
"Future time we hold in fee!

"If each bear, each quadruped,
Held with me a like ideal,
With our whole united force
We the tyrant might engage.

"Compact then the boar should make
With the horse—the elephant
Curve his trunk in comradeship
Round the valiant ox's horns.

"Bear and wolf of every shade,
Goat and ape, the rabbit, too.
Let them for the common cause

Labour—and the world is ours!

"Union! union! is the need
Of our times! For singly we
Fall as slaves, but joined as one
We shall overcome our lords.

"Union! union! Victory!
We shall overthrow the reign
Of such tyranny and found
One great Kingdom of the Brutes.

"And its first great law shall be
For God's creatures one and all
Equal rights—no matter what
Be their faith, or hide or smell.

"Strict equality! Each ass
May become Prime Minister;
On the other hand the lion
Shall bear corn unto the mill.

"And the dog? Alas, 'tis true
He's a very servile cur,
Just because for ages man
Like a dog has treated him.

"Yet in our Free State shall he
Once again enjoy his rights—
Rights most unassailable—
Thus ennobled be the dog.

"Yea, the very Jews shall win
All the rights of citizens,
By the law made equal with
Every other mammal free.

"One thing only be denied them!
Dancing in the market-place;
This amendment I shall make
In the interests of my art.

"For they lack all sense of style;
All plasticity of limb
Lacks that race. Full surely they
Would debauch the public taste."

CANTO VII

Gloomy in his gloomy cave,
In the circle of his home,
Crouches Troll, the Foe of Man,
As he growls and champs his jaws.

"Men, O crafty, pert *canaille*!
Smile away! That mighty hour
Dawns wherein we shall be freed
From your bondage and your smiles!

"Most offensive was to me
That same twitching bitter-sweet
Of the lips—the smiles of men
I found unendurable!

"When in every visage white
I beheld that fatal spasm,
Then did anger seize my bowels
And I felt a hideous qualm.

"For the smiling lips of men
More insultingly declare,
Even than their lips avouch,
All their insolence of soul.

"And they smile forever! Even
When all decency demands
Gravity—as in the moments
Of love's solemn mysteries.

"Yea, they smile forever. Even
In their dances!—desecrate
Thus this high and noble art
Which a sacred cult should be.

"Ah, the dance in olden days
Was a pious act of faith,
When the priests in solemn round
Turned about their holy shrines.

"Thus before the Covenant's
Sacred Ark King David danced.
Dancing then was worship too,—
It was praying with the legs!

"So did I regard my dance
When before the people all
In the market-place I danced
And was cheered by every soul.

"This applause, I grant you, oft
Made me feel content at heart;
Sweet it is from grudging foes
Admiration thus to win!

"Yet despite their rapture they
Still would smile and smile! My art—
Even that proved vain to save
Them from base frivolity!"

CANTO VIII

Many a virtuous citizen
Smells unpleasantly the while
Ducal knaves are lavendered
Or a-reek with ambergris.

There are many virgin souls
Redolent of greenest soap;
Vice will often lave herself
In rose attar top to toe.

Therefore, gentle reader, pray,
Do not lift your nose in air
Should Troll's cavern fail to rouse
Memories of Arabia's spice.

Bide with me within this reek,
'Mid these turbid odours foul,
Whence unto his son our hero
Speaks, as from a misty cloud:

"Child, my child, the last begot
Of my loins, thy single ear
Snuggle close against the snout
Of thy father, and give heed!

"Oh, beware man's mode of thought;
It destroys both flesh and soul,
For amongst all mankind never
Shalt thou find one worthy man.

"E'en the Germans, once the best,
Even Tuiskion's sons,
Our dear cousins primitive,
Even they have grown effete.

"Godless, faithless have they grown;
Atheism now they preach.
Child, my child, oh, guard thee 'gainst

Feuerbach and Bauer too!

"Never be an atheist!
Monster void of reverence!
For a great Creator reared
All the mighty Universe!

"And the sun and moon on high,
And the stars—the stars with tails
Even as the tailless ones—
Are reflections of His power.

"In the depths of sea and land
Ring the echoes of His fame,
And each creature yields Him praise
For His glory and His might.

"E'en the tiny silver louse
Which within some pilgrim's beard
Shares his earthly pilgrimage,
Sings to Him a song of praise!

"High upon his golden throne
In yon splendid tent of stars,
Clad in cosmic majesty,
Sits a titan polar bear.

"Spotless, gleaming white as snow
Is his fur; his head is decked
With a crown of diamonds
Blazing through the central vault.

"In his face bide harmony
And the silent deeds of thought,
And obedient to his sceptre
All the planets chime and sing.

"At his feet sit holy bears,
Saints who suffered on the Earth,
Meekly. In their paws they hold
Splendid palms of martyrdom.

"Ever and anon they leap
To their feet as though aroused
By the Holy Ghost, and lo!
In a festal dance they join!

"'Tis a dance where saintly gifts
Cover up defects of style,—
Dance in which the very soul
Seeks to leap from out its skin!

"I, unworthy Troll, shall I

Ever such salvation share?
Shall I ever from this drear
Vale of tears ascend to joy?

"Shall I, drunk with Heaven's draught,
In that tent of stars above,
Dance before the Master's throne
With a halo and a palm?"

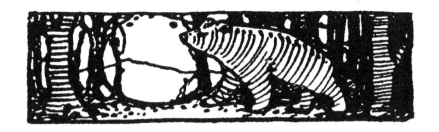

CANTO IX

As the noble negro king
Of our Freiligrath protrudes
From his dusky mouth his long
Scarlet tongue in scorn and rage, —

Even so the moon now peers
Out of darkling clouds. The sad,
Sleepless waterfalls forever
Roar into the brooding night.

Atta Troll upon the crest
Of his well-beloved cliff
Stands alone, and now he howls
Down the wind and the abyss:

"Yea, a bear am I—even he,
Even he whom you have named
Bruin, growler, shag-coat too,
And such other titles vile.

"Yea, a bear am I—that same
Boorish animal you know;
That gross, trampling brute am I
Of your sly and crafty smiles!

"Of your wit am I the mark;
I'm the bugbear—him with whom
Every wicked child you frighten
In the silence of the night.

"Yea, I am that clumsy butt
Of your nursery tales—aloud
Will I shout that name forever
Through the scurvy world of men.

"Oyez! Oyez! I'm a bear
Unashamed of my descent,
Just as proud as if my forbear
Had been Moses Mendelsohn."

CANTO X

Lo, two figures, wild and sullen,
Gliding, sliding on all fours,
Break a path at dead of night
Through a wood of gloomy pines.

It is Atta Troll the Sire,
One-Ear too, his youngest son,
And they halt within a clearing
By a stone of bloody rites.

"This same stone," growled Atta Troll,
"Is a shrine where Druids once
Slaughtered wretched human wights
In dark Superstition's days.

"Oh! what frightful horrors these!
When I think of them, my fur
Lifts along my back! To praise
God they drenched the soil in blood!

"Certes, men have now become
More enlightened. Now no more
Do they slaughter in their zeal
For celestial interests.

"'Tis no longer holy rage,
Ecstasy nor madness sheer,
But self-love alone that urges
Them to slaughter and to crime.

"Now for worldly goods they strive,
Day by day and year by year.
It is one eternal war;
Each goes robbing for himself.

"When the common goods of all
Fall into the hands of one,
Straight of Rights of Property

He will prate and Ownership.

"Property! Just Ownership?
Property is theft! O lies!
Craft and folly!—such a mixture
Man alone would dare invent.

"Never yet did Nature make
Properties, for pocketless
We are born into the world—
Who hath pockets in his pelt?

"None of us was ever born
With such little sacks devised
In our outer hides and skins
To enable us to steal!

"Only man, that creature smooth
Who in alien wool is garbed
Artfully, in artful wise
Made himself such pockets too.

"Pockets! as unnatural
As is property itself,
Or that law of have-and-hold.
Men are only pocket-thieves!

"Flamingly I hate them! Thee
All my hatred I bequeath.
Oh, my son, upon this shrine
Shalt thou swear eternal hate!

"Be the mortal foeman thou
Of th' oppressor, unforgiving
To thy very end of days!
Swear it—swear it here, my son!"

And the youngster swore as once
Hannibal. The moonbeams bleak
Yellowed on the bloodstone hoary
And that brace of misanthropes.

Later shall our harp record
How the young bear kept his faith
And his plighted oath,—for him
Shall our epic strings be strung.

With regard to Atta Troll,
Let us leave him for a space,
So we may the surer smite
Him with our unerring ball.

Traitor to Humanity!

Thou art judged, the sentence writ.
Of *lèse-majesté* thou'rt guilty,
And to-morrow sees the chase.

CANTO XI

Like to sleepy dancing-girls
Lift the mountains white and cold,
Standing in their skirts of mist
Flaunted by the winds of morn.

Yet full soon their breasts shall glow
To the sun-god's burning kiss,
He shall tear the clinging veils
And illume their beauty nude.

In the early dawn had I
With Lascaro sallied forth
On a bear-hunt and the noon
Saw us at the Pont d'Espagne.

Thus is named the bridge that leads
From the land of France to Spain,
To barbarians of the West,
Centuries behind the times.

Full ten centuries they lie
From all modern thought removed,
And my own barbarians
Of the East—not more than two.

Lingering and loth I left
The all-hallowed soil of France,
Left great Freedom's motherland
And the women that I love.

Midmost of the Pont d'Espagne
Sat a Spaniard. Misery
Lurked within his tattered cape;
Misery lurked within his eyes.

With his bony fingers he
Plucked an ancient mandolin
Full of discord shrill which echoed

Mockingly from out the gulch.

Then betimes he leaned aslant
O'er the depths and laughed aloud,
Tinkled then in maddest wise
As he sang his little song:

"In my very heart of heart
There's a tiny golden table,
And about this golden table
Four small golden chairs are set.

"Seated on these golden chairs,
Little dames with darts of gold
In their hair are playing cards—
Clara wins at every game.

"Yes, she wins and smiles in glee.
Clara, oh, within my heart,
Thou can'st never fail to win,
For thou holdest all the trumps!"

On I wandered and I spoke
Thus unto myself. How strange!
Lunacy itself sits there
Singing on the road to Spain.

Is this madman not a sign
Of how nations trade in thought?
Or is he his native land's
Wild and crazy title-page?

Twilight sank before we came
To a wretched old *posada*
Where *podrida*—favourite dish!
Steamed within a dirty pot.

There *garbanzos* did I eat
Huge and hard as musket-balls,
Which not e'en a native Teuton,
Bred on dumplings, could digest.

And my bed was of a piece,
With the cooking. Insects vile
Dotted it. Oh, surely these
Are the grimmest foes of man!

Far more fearful than the wrath
Of a thousand elephants,
Is one small and angry bug
Crawling o'er thy lowly couch.

Helpless thou against its bite—

That is bad enough!—but worse
Evil comes if it be crushed
And its horrid smell released.

All Life's terrors we may taste
In the war with vermin waged,
Vermin well-equipped with stinks,
And in duels with a bug.

CANTO XII

How they rave, the blessèd bards—
Even the tamest! how they sing,—
How they do protest that Nature
Is a mighty fane of God!

One great fane whose splendours all
Of the Maker's glory tell;
Sun and moon and stars they vow
Hang as lamps within the dome.

Yet concede, most worthy folk,
That this mighty temple hath
Most uncomfortable stairs,
Stairs most villainously bad!

All this climbing up and down,
Escalading, jumping o'er
Boulders—how it tires me
Both in spirit and in legs!

By my side Lascaro strode,
Like a taper long and pale—
Never speaks he, never laughs—
He the witch's lifeless son.

For they say Lascaro died
Many years ago—his mother's,—
Old Uraka's,—magic draughts
Gave to him a seeming life.

These confounded temple steps!
How it chanced that I escaped
With whole vertebræ will puzzle
Me until my dying day.

How the torrents foamed and roared!
Through the pines how lashed the wind
Till they groaned! Then suddenly

Burst the clouds! O weather vile!

In a fisherman's poor hut
Close by Lac de Gaube we gained
Shelter and a mess of trout—
Dish divine and glorious!

In his padded arm-chair there
Sat the ancient ferryman,
Ill and grey. His nieces sweet
Like two angels tended him.

Plumpest angels, Flemish quite,
As if out of Rubens' frame
They had leaped, with golden locks,
Sparkling eyes of limpid blue,

Dimples in each ruddy cheek
Where bright mischief peered and hid,
And with limbs robust and lithe,
Waking both desire and fear.

Sweet and bonny creatures they
Who disputed prettily
Which might prove the sweetest draught
To their ancient, ailing charge.

If one proffers him a brew
Made of linden-flower tea,
Then the other tempts him with
Possets made of elder-blooms.

"I will swallow none of this!"
Cried the greyhead, sorely tried,
"Bring me wine so that my guest
May have worthy drink with me!"

If this stuff was really wine
Which I drank at Lac de Gaube—
Who can tell? My countrymen
Would have dubbed it sweetish beer.

Vilely smelled the wine-skin too,
Fashioned from a black goat's hide.
But the old man drank and drank
And grew jubilant and gay.

Of banditti tales he told
And of smugglers, merry men
Who still ply their goodly trades
Freely in the Pyrenees.

Many ancient stories, too,

He recited, as of wars
'Twixt the giants and the bears
In the grey primeval days.

For it seems the bears and ogres
Waged a war for mastery
Of these ranges and these vales
Long ere man came wandering in.

Startled then at sight of men
All the giants fled the land;—
Only tiny brains were housed
In their huge, unwieldy heads!

It is also said these dolts,
When they reached the ocean-shore
Where the azure skies lay glassed
In the watery plains below,

Fondly fancied that the sea
Must be Heaven. In they plunged
All in reckless confidence,
And in watery graves were gulfed.

Now the bears are slain by man,
And each year their number grows
Smaller, smaller, till at last
None shall roam within the hills.

"And," the old man cackled, "thus
On this Earth must one yield room
To the other—after man
We shall have a reign of dwarfs.

"Tiny and most clever wights
Toiling in the bowels of Earth,
Busy little folk that gather
Riches from Earth's golden veins.

"I have seen their rounded heads
Peering out of rabbit-holes
In the moonlight—and I shook
As I thought of coming days.

"Yes, I dread the golden power
Of these mites. Our sons, I fear,
Will like stupid giants plunge
Straight into some watery heaven."

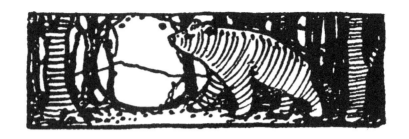

CANTO XIII

In the cauldron of the cliffs
Lies the deep and inky lake.
And from heaven the solemn stars
Peer upon us. Night and stillness.

Night and stillness. Beat of oars.
Like a rippling mystery
Swims our boat. The nieces twain
Serve in place of ferrymen.

Swift and blithe they row. Their arms
Sometimes shine from out the night,
And on their white skins the stars
Gleam and on large eyes of blue.

At my side Lascaro sits
Pale and mute as is his wont,
And I shudder at the thought:
Is Lascaro really dead?

Or perchance 'tis I am dead?
I, perchance, am drifting down
With these spectral passengers
To the icy realm of shades?

Can this lake be Styx's dark,
Sullen flood? Hath Proserpine,
In the absence of her Charon
Sent her maids to fetch me down?

Nay, not yet my days are done!
Unextinguished in my soul
Still the living flame of life,
Leaps and blazes, glows and sings.

And these girls who swing their oars
Merrily, and splash me too,
Laugh and grin with mischief rare
As the drops upon me flash.

Ah, these wenches fresh and strong,
Surely they could never be
Ghostly hell-cats, nor the maids
Of the dark queen Proserpine.

So that I might be assured
Of the girls' reality,
And unto myself might prove
My own honest flesh and blood,—

On their rosy dimples I
Swiftly pressed my eager lips,
And to this conclusion came:
Lo, I kiss; therefore I live!

When we reached the shore, again
Did I kiss these bonny maids,—
Kisses were the only coin
Which in payment they would take.

CANTO XIV

Joyous in the golden air
Lift the purple mountain heights
Where a daring hamlet clings
Like a nest against the steep.

Wearily I climbed and climbed.
When at last I stood aloft,
Then I found the old birds flown
And the fledglings left behind.

Pretty lads and lassies small
With their little heads half hid
In their white and scarlet caps,
Played at bridals in the mart.

Neither stay nor halt they brooked,
And the little love-lorn Prince
Of the Mice knelt down at once
To the Cat-King's daughter fair.

Hapless Prince! At last he's wed
To the Princess. How she scolds!
Bites him and devours him—
Hapless mouse!—thus ends the play.

That entire day I spent
With the children, and we talked
Cosily. They longed to know
Who I was? and what my trade?

"Germany, my dears," I spoke,
"Is my native country's name—
Bears are all too common there,
So I took to hunting bears!

"Many a bear-pelt have I pulled
Over many a bearish head,
Though, 'tis true, I sometimes got
Damage from their bearish paws.

"But at last I felt disgust
Of this strife with ill-licked boors
In my blessèd land—I grew
Weary of these daily moils.

"So in quest of nobler game,
I at last have come to you;
I shall try my little strength
'Gainst the mighty Atta Troll.

"Worthy of me is this noble
Foe. In Germany, alas!
Many a battle did I win,
Most ashamed of victory."

When I left, the little folk
Danced about me in a ring,
And in sweetest wise they sang:
"Girofflino! Girofflett'!"

And the youngest of them all
Stepped before me quick and pert,
And four times she curtsied low
As she sang in silver tones:

"Curtsies two I give the King,
Should I meet him. And the Queen,
Should I meet her, then I give
Curtsies three unto the Queen.

"But should I the devil meet
With his fiery eyes and horns,
I will make him curtsies four—
Girofflino! Girofflett'!"

"Girofflino! Girofflett'!"
Shouts once more the mocking band,
And around me swings the gay
Ring-o'-roses with its song.

As I scrambled down the slopes,
After me in echoes sweet,
Came these words in bird-like strains:
"Girofflino! Girofflett'!"

CANTO XV

Hulking and enormous cliffs
Of deformed and twisted shapes
Look on me like petrified
Monsters of primeval times.

Strange! the dingy clouds above
Drift like doubles bred of mist,
Like some silly counterfeit
Of these savage shapes of stone.

In the distance roars the fall;
Through the fir trees howls the wind!
'Tis a sound implacable
And as fatal as despair.

Lone and dreadful lies the waste
And the black daws sit in swarms
On the bleached and rotten pines,
Flapping with their weary wings.

At my side Lascaro strides
Pale and silent—I myself
Must like sorry madness look
By dire Death accompanied.

'Tis a wild and desert place.
Curst perchance? I seem to see
On the crippled roots of yonder
Tree a crimson smear of blood.

This tree shades a little hut
Cowering humbly in the earth,
And the wretched roof of thatch
Pleads for pity in your sight.

Cagots are the denizens
Of this hut—the last remains
Of a tribe which sunk in darkness
Bides its bitter destiny.

In the heart of every Basque
You will find a rooted hate
Of the Cagots. 'Tis a foul
Relic of the days of faith.

In the minster at Bagnères
You may see a narrow grille,
Once the door, the sexton told me,
Which the herded Cagots used.

In that day all other gates
Were forbidden them. They crawled
Like to thieves into the blest
House of God to worship there.

There these wretched beings sat
On their lowly stools and prayed,
Parted as by leprosy,
From all other worshippers.

But the hallowed lamps of this
Later century burn bright,
And their light destroys the black
Shadows of that cruel age!

While Lascaro waited there,
Entered I the lonely hut
Of the Cagot, and I clasped
Straight his hand in brotherhood.

Likewise did I kiss his child
Which unto the shrivelled breast
Of his wife clung fast and sucked
Like some spider sick and starved.

CANTO XVI

Shouldst thou see these mountain peaks
From the distance thou wouldst think
That with gold and purple they
Flamed in splendour to the sun.

But at closer hand their pomp
Vanishes. Earth's glories thus
With their myriad light-effects
Still beguile us artfully.

What to thee seemed blue and gold
Is, alas, but idle snow,
Idle snow which, lone and drear,
Bores itself in solitude.

There upon the heights I heard
How the hapless crackling snow
Cried aloud its pallid grief
To the cold and heartless wind:

"Ah," it sobbed, "how slow the hours
Crawl within this awful waste!
All these many endless hours,
Like eternities of ice!

"Woe is me, poor snow! I would
I had never seen these peaks—
Might I but in vales have fallen
Where a myriad flowers bloom!

"To some little brook would I
Then have melted, and some maid—
Fairest of the land! with smiles
Would in me have laved her face.

"Yea, perchance, I might have fared
To the sea and changed betimes
To a pearl and gleamed at last

In some royal coronet!"

When I heard this plaint, I spake:
"Dearest Snow, indeed I doubt
Whether such a brilliant fate
Had been thine within the world.

"Comfort take. Few, few, indeed,
Ever grow to pearls. No doubt
Thou hadst fallen in the mire
And become a clod of mud."

As in kindly wise I spoke
Thus unto the joyless snow,
Came a shot—and from the skies
Plunged a hawk of brownish wing.

It was just a hunter's joke
Of Lascaro's. But his face
Was as ever stark and grim,
And his rifle barrel smoked.

Silently he tore a plume
From the hawk's erected tail,
Stuck it in his pointed hat
And resumed his silent way.

'Twas an eerie sight to see
How his shadow black and thin
With the nodding feather moved
O'er the slopes of drifted snow.

CANTO XVII

Lo, a valley like a street!
'Tis the Hollow Way of Ghosts:
Dizzily the cloven crags
Tower up on every side.

There upon the sheerest slope
Hangs Uraka's little shack
Like some outpost over chaos—
Thither fared her son and I.

In a secret dumb-show speech
He took counsel with his dam,
How great Atta Troll might best
Be ensnared and safely slain.

We had found his mighty spoor.
Never more canst thou escape
From our hands! thine earthly days
All are numbered—Atta Troll!

Never could I well determine
If Uraka, ancient hag,
Was in truth a potent witch,
As within these Pyrenees

It was rumoured. But I know
That in truth her very looks
Were suspicious. Most suspicious
Were her red and running eyes.

Evil is her look and slant.
It is said whene'er she stares
At some hapless cow, its milk
Dries, its udder withers straight.

It is said that stroking with
Her thin fingers, many a kid
She had slaughtered, many a huge
Ox had stricken unto death.

Oft within the local court
For such crimes arraigned she stood,
But the Justice of the Peace
Was a true Voltairean.

Quite a modern worldling he,
Shallow and devoid of faith,—
So the plaintiffs he dismissed
Both in mockery and scorn.

The alleged official trade
Of Uraka's honest quite,
For she deals in mountain-herbs
And in birds that she has stuffed.

Her entire hut was crammed
With such relics. Horrible
Was the smell of cuckoo-flowers,
Fungi, henbane, elder-blooms.

There a fine array of hawks
To advantage was displayed,
All with pinions stretching wide
And with grim enormous bills.

Was it but the breath of these
Maddening plants that turned my brain?
Still the vision of these birds
Filled me with the strangest thoughts.

These perchance are mortal wights,
Bound by sorcery in this
Miserable state as birds
Stuffed and most disconsolate.

Sad, pathetic is their stare,
Yet it hath impatience too,
And, methinks at times they cast
Sidelong glances at the witch.

She, Uraka, ancient, grim,
Crouches low beside her son,
Mute Lascaro near the fire
Where the twain are casting slugs.

Casting that same fateful ball
Whereby Atta Troll was slain.
How the lurching firelight flares
O'er the witch's features gaunt!

Ceaselessly, yet silently
Move her thin and quivering lips.
Are those magic spells she murmurs

That the balls may travel true?

Now and then she nods and titters
To her son. But he is deep
In the business of the casts
And sits silently as Death.

Overcome by fevered fears,
Yearning for the cooler air,
To the window then I strode
And looked down the gulches dim.

All that in that midnight hour
I beheld, all that will I
Faithfully and featly tell
In the canto that shall follow.

CANTO XVIII

'Twas the night before Saint John's,
In the fullness of the moon,
When that wild and spectral hunt
Fills the Hollow Way of Ghosts.

From the window of Uraka's
Little cabin I could see
All that mighty host of wraiths
As it drifted through the gorge.

Yea, a goodly place was mine
Wherefrom I might well behold
The tremendous spectacle
Of the raised, carousing dead.

Cracking whips, hallo! hurrah!
Neigh of horses, bark of dogs,
Laughter, blare of huntsmen's horns—
How the tumult echoed there!

Dashing in advance there came
Stags and boars adventurous
In a solid pack; behind
Charged a wild and merry rout.

Huntsmen come from many zones
And from many ages too.
Charles the Tenth rode close beside
Nimrod the Assyrian.

High upon their snowy steeds
They charged onward. Then on foot
Came the whips with hounds in leash
And the pages with the links.

Many in that maddened horde
Seemed familiar—yon knight
Gleaming all in golden mail,—

Surely was King Arthur's self!

And Lord Ogier the Dane
In chain-armour shining green,
Truly close resemblance bore
To some mighty frog forsooth!

Many a hero I beheld
Of the gleaming world of thought;
Wolfgang Goethe straight I knew
By the sparkling of his eyes.

Being damned by Hengstenberg,
In his grave no peace he finds,
So with pagan blazonry
Gallops down the chase of Life.

By the glamour of his smile
Did I know the mighty Will
Whom the Puritans once cursed
Like our Goethe, — yet must he,

Luckless sinner, in this host
Ride a charger black as coal.
Close beside him on an ass
Rode a mortal and — great heavens!

By the weary mien of prayer
And the snowy night-cap too,
And the terror of his soul,
Francis Horn I recognized.

Commentaries he composed
On that great and cosmic child,
Shakespeare — therefore at his side
He must ride through thick and thin.

Lo, poor silent Francis rides,
He who scarcely dared to walk,
He who only stirred himself
At tea-tables and at prayers.

Surely all the oldish maids
Who indulged him in his ease,
Will be startled when they hear
Of his riding rough and free.

When the gallop faster grows,
Then great William glances down
On his commentator meek
Jogging onward on his ass.

To the saddle clinging tight,

Fainting in his terror sheer,
Yet unto his author loyal
In his death as in his life.

Many ladies there I saw,
In that crazy train of ghosts,
Many lovely nymphs with forms
Slender with the grace of youth.

On their steeds they sat astride
Mythologically nude!
Though their tresses thick and long
Fell like cloaks of stranded gold.

Garlands rustled on their heads
And they swung their laurelled staves,
Bending back in reckless ways,
Full of joyous insolence.

Mediæval maids I saw
Buttoned high unto the chin,
On their saddles seated slant,
Poising falcons on their wrists.

Like a burlesque, from behind
On their hacks and skinny nags
Came a rout of merry wenches,
Most extravagantly garbed.

And each face, though lovely quite,
Bore a trace of impudence;
Madly would they shriek and yell,
Puffing up their painted cheeks.

How this tumult echoed there!
Laughter, blare of huntsmen's horns;
Neigh of horses, bark of dogs,
Crack of whips! hallo! hurrah!

CANTO XIX

But like Beauty's clover-leaf,
In the very midst arose
Three fair women. I shall never
Their majestic forms forget!

Well I knew the first! Her head
Glittered with the crescent moon.
Haughty, like some ivory statue
Sat the goddess on her steed.

And her fluttering tunic fell
Loose about her hips and breasts,
And the torchlight and the moon
Laved with love her snowy limbs.

Marble seemed her very face
And like marble cold. How dread
Was the pallor and the chill
Of that stern and noble front!

But within her dusky eye
Smouldered a mysterious,
Cruel and enticing fire
Which devoured my poor soul.

What a change has come o'er Dian
Since in outraged chastity
She smote Actæon to a stag
As a quarry for his hounds!

Doth she now requite this crime
In this gallant company,
Riding like some ghostly mortal
Through the bleak, nocturnal air?

Late did passion wake in her
But for that the stronger burns,
And within her eyes its flames

Gleam like fiercest brands of hell.

For those vanished times she grieves
When the men were beautiful;
Now in quantity perchance,
She forgets their quality.

At her side a fair one rode—
Fair, but not by Grecian lines
Was she fair; for all her features
Shone with wondrous Celtic glow.

'Twas Abunda, fairy queen,
Whom to know I could not fail
By the sweetness of her smile
And the madness of her laugh!

Full and rosy was her face,
Like the faces limned by Greuze;
And from out her heart-shaped mouth
Flashed the splendour of her teeth!

All the winds made dalliance
With her robe of azure blue,
And such shoulders never I
In my wildest dreams beheld.

I was almost moved to leap
From the window for a kiss;
This had been sheer folly, true,
Ending in a broken neck!

Ah, and she, she would have laughed
If within that awful gulf
I had fallen at her feet;—
Laughter such as this I know!

And the third fair phantom, she
Who so moved my errant heart,—
Was this but some female fiend
Like the other figures twain?

Whether devil this or saint
Know I not. With women, ah,
None can ever know where saint
Ends nor where the fiend begins.

All the magic of the East
Lay within her glowing face,
And her dress brought memories
Of Scheherazadê's tales.

Lips as red as pomegranates

And a curved nose lily white,
Limbs as slender and as cool
As some green oasis-palm.

From her palfrey white she leaned,
Flanked by giant Moors who trod
Close beside the queenly dame
Holding up the golden reins.

Of most royal blood was she,
She the Queen of old Judea,
She great Herod's lovely wife,
She who craved the Baptist's head.

For this crimson crime was she
Banned and cursed. Now in this chase
Must she ride, a wandering spook,
Till the dawn of Judgment Day.

Still within her hands she bears
That deep charger with the head
Of the Prophet, still she kisses—
Kisses it with fiery lips.

For she loved the Prophet once,
Though the Bible naught reveals,
Yet her blood-stained love lives on
Storied in her people's hearts.

How might else a man declare
All the longing of this lady?
Would a woman crave the head
Of a man she did not love?

She perchance was slightly vexed
With her darling, and was moved
To behead him, but when she
On the trencher saw his head,

Then she wept and lost her wits,
Dying in love's madness straight.
(What! Love's madness? pleonasm!
Love itself is madness still!)

Rising nightly from her grave,
To this frenzied hunt she hies,
In her hands the gory head
Which with feline joy she flings

High into the air betimes,
Laughing like a wanton child,
Cleverly she catches it
Like some idle rubber ball.

As she swept past me she bowed
Most coquettishly and looked
On me with her melting eyes,
So that all my heart was stirred.

Thrice that rout raged up and down
Past my window, then did she,
Ah, most beautiful of shades!
Greet me with her precious smile.

Even when the pageant dimmed
And the tumult silent grew
In my brain, that smiling face
Shone and beckoned on and on.

All that night I tossed and turned
My o'erwearied limbs on straw,
Musty straw. No feather-beds
In Uraka's hut I found!

And I mused: what might this mean,
This mysterious beckoning?
Why, Oh, why, Herodias,
Held thy look such tenderness?

CANTO XX

Sunrise. Golden arrows dart
Through the pallid ranks of mist
Till they redden as with wounds
And dissolve in shining light.

Now hath triumph come to Day
And the gleaming conqueror
In his blinding glory treads
O'er the ridges and the peaks.

All the merry bands of birds
Twitter in their hidden nests,
And the scent of plants arises
Like a psalm of odours rare.

At the early glint of day
Down the valley we had gone.
While Lascaro dumb and dour
Followed up the bear-tracks dim,

I with musings sought to slay
Time, but tired soon I grew
Of my musings,—drear, ah, drear!
Were my thoughts and void of joy.

Weary, joyless, down I sank
On a bank of softest moss
'Neath a great and kingly ash
Where a little spring gushed forth.

This with wondrous voice beguiled
All my wayward mood until
Thought and thinking vanished both
In the music of the spring.

Mighty longings seized me then,
Madness, dreams and death-desires,
Longings for those splendid queens

Riding in that ghostly throng.

Oh, ye lovely shapes of night,
Banished by the rose of dawn,
Whither, tell me, have ye fled,
Whither have ye flown by day?

Somewhere 'neath old temple-ruins
In the wide Romagna hid,
It is said Diana flees
The dominion of the Christ.

Only in the midnight gloom,
Dare she venture forth, but then
How she joys the merry chase
And the pagan sports of old!

Fay Abunda also fears
All these sallow Nazarenes,
So by day she hides herself
Deep in secret Avalon.

For this sacred island lies
In the still and silent sea
Of Romanticism, whither
None save wingèd steeds may go.

There no anchor Care may drop,
Never there do steamships touch,
Bringing loads of Philistines
With tobacco-pipes, to stare.

Never does that dismal, dull
Ring of bells this stillness break—
That atrocious bumm-bamm sound
Which all gentle fairies hate.

There, abloom with lasting youth
In unbroken joyfulness,
Lives that merry-hearted dame,
Golden-locked Abunda fair.

Laughing there she strolls between
Huge sun-flowers drenched with light,
Followed by her retinue
Of unworldly Paladins.

Ah, but thou, Herodias,
Say, where art thou? Ah, I know!
Thou art dead and buried deep
By Jerusholayim's walls!

Corpse-like is thy sleep by day

In thy marble coffin laid,
But at midnight dost thou wake
To the crack of whips! hurrah!

With Abunda, Dian, too,
Dost thou join the headlong plunge
And the blithesome hunter rout
Fleeing from all cross and care.

What companions rare and blithe!
Might but I, Herodias,
Ride at night through forests dark,
I would gallop at thy side!

For of all I love thee most!
More than any goddess Grecian,
More than any northern fay,
Do I love thee, Jewess dead!

Yea, I love thee most! 'Tis true,
By the trembling of my soul!
Love me too and be my sweet,—
Loveliest Herodias!

Love me too and be my love!
Fling that gory block-head far
With its trencher. Sweeter dishes
I shall give thee to enjoy.

Am not I thy proper knight
Whom thou seekest? What care I
If perchance thou'rt dead and damned—
Prejudices I have none!

Is my own salvation not
In a parlous state? And oft
Do I question if my life
Still be linked with human lives.

Take me, take me as thy knight,
Thine own *cavalier servente*;
I will bear thy silken robe
And each wayward mood of thine.

Every night beside thee, love,
With this crazy horde I'll ride,
And we'll kiss and thou shalt laugh
At my quips and merry pranks.

I will help thee speed the hours
Of the night. And yet by day
All my joy shall pass;—in tears
I shall sit upon thy grave.

Aye, by day will I sit down
In the dust of kingly vaults,
At the grave of my belovèd
By Jerusholayim's walls!

Then the grey Jews passing by
Will imagine that I mourn
The destruction of thy temple
And thy gates, Jerusholayim.

CANTO XXI

Shipless Argonauts are we,
Foot loose in the mighty hills,
But instead of golden fleece
We seek Bruin's shaggy hide.

Naught but sorry devils twain,
Heroes of a modern cut,
And no classic bard will ever
Make us live within his song!

Even though we suffered dire
Hardships! What torrential rains
Fell upon us at the peak
Where was neither tree nor cab!

Cloudbursts! Heaven's dykes were down!
And in bucketsful it poured—
Jason, lost on Colchis bleak,
Suffered no such shower-bath!

"Six-and-thirty kings I'll give
Just for one umbrella now!"
So I cried. Umbrella none
Was I offered in that flood.

Weary unto death and glum,
Wet as drownèd rats, we came
Back unto the witch's hut
In the middle of the night.

There beside the glowing hearth
Sat Uraka with a comb,
Toiling o'er her swollen pug;—
Him she quickly flung aside

As we entered. First my couch
She prepared, then bent to loose
From my feet the *espardillos*,—
Footgear comfortless and rude!

Helped me to disrobe, — she drew
Off my pantaloons which clung
To my legs as close and tight
As the friendship of a fool.

"Oh, a dressing-gown! I'd give
Six-and-thirty kings," I cried,
"For a dry one!" — as my shirt,
Wringing wet, began to steam.

Shivering, with chattering teeth,
There I stood beside the hearth,
Till the fire drowsed me quite,
Then upon the straw I sank.

Sleepless but with blinking eyes
Peered I at the witch who crouched
By the fire with her son's
Body spread upon her lap.

Upright at her side the pug
Stood, and in his clumsy paws,
Very cleverly and tight,
Held aloft a little jar.

From this did Uraka take
Reddish fat and salved therewith
Swift Lascaro's ribs and breast
With her thin and trembling hands.

And she hummed a lullaby
In a high and nasal tone
As she rubbed him with the salve
'Midst the crackling of the fire.

Sere and bony like a corpse
Lay the son upon the lap
Of his mother; opened wide
Stared his pale and tragic eyes.

Is he really dead, this man?
Kept alive by mother-love?
Nightly by the witch-fat potent
Salved into a magic life?

Oh, that strange, strange fever-sleep!
In which all my limbs grew stiff
As if fettered, yet each sense,
Overwrought, waked horribly!

How that smell of hellish herbs
Plagued me! Musing in my woe,
Long I thought where had I once

Smelled such odours?—but in vain.

How the wind within the flue
Wrought me terror! Like the sobs
Of some parchèd soul it rang—
Or some well-remembered voice!

But these stuffed birds standing guard
On a board above my head,
These grim birds tormented me
Far beyond all other things!

Slowly, gruesomely they moved
Their accursèd wings and bent
Low to me with monstrous bills,
Bills like human noses huge.

Where had I such noses seen?
Well, mayhap in Hamburg once,
Or in Frankfort's ghetto dim;
Memory smote me harshly then.

But at last did slumber quite
Overcome me and in place
Of such waking phantoms crept
Wholesome and unbroken dreams.

And within my dream the hut
Quickly to a ball-room changed,
High on lofty pillars borne
And illumed by chandeliers.

There invisible musicians
Played from "Robert le Diable"
That atrocious dance of nuns
As I promenaded there.

But at last the portals wide
Open and with stately step
Slowly in the hall appear
Guests most wonderful and strange.

Every one a bear or spectre!
Striding upright every bear
Leads an apparition wrapped
In a white and gleaming shroud.

Coupled in this wise, each pair
Up and down began to waltz
Through the hall. O strangest sight!
Fit for laughter and for fear!

How those plump old animals

Panted in the paces set
By those filmy shapes of air
Whirling gracefully and light!

Pitiless, the harried beasts
Thus were borne along until
Their deep panting overdroned
Even the orchestral bass!

When betimes the couples crashed
In collision, then each bear
Gave the pushing spectre straight
Hearty kicks upon the rump.

Sometimes in the tumult too
When the cerements fell away
From each white and muffled head,—
Lo! a grinning skull appeared!

But at last with shattering blare
Yelled the horns, the cymbals clashed
And the thunder of the drums
Brought about the gallopade.

But the end of this, alas,
Came not to my dreams. For, lo,
One most clumsy bear trod full
On my corns—I shrieked and woke!

CANTO XXII

Phœbus in his solar coach,
Whipping up his steeds of flame,
Had traversed the middle part
Of his journey through the skies,

Whilst in sleep I lay a-dream
With the goblins and the bears
Winding like mad arabesques
Through my slack and heated brain.

When I wakened it was noon,
And I found myself alone,
Since my hostess and Lascaro
For the chase had left at dawn.

There was no one save the pug
In the hovel. There he stood
By the hearth beside the pot
Holding in his paws a spoon.

Clever pug! well disciplined!
Lest the steaming soup boil over,
Swift he stirred it round and round,
Skimming off the foam and scum.

But—am I bewitchèd too?
Or does fever smoulder still
In my brain? For scarce can I
Trust my ears. The pug-dog speaks!

Aye, he speaks in homely strains
Of the Swabian dialect,
Deeply sunk in thought, he cries,
As it were within a dream:

"Woe is me—a Swabian bard,
Banned in exile must I grieve
In a pug-dog's cursèd shape

Guardian of a witch's pot.

"What a base and hideous crime
Is this sorcery! My fate
Ah, how tragic! I, a man,
In the body of a dog!

"Had I but remained at home
With my jolly comrades true—
No vile sorcerers are they!
And their spells no man need fear.

"Had I but remained at home
At Karl Meyer's—with the sweet
Noodles of the Vaterland
And good honest metzel-soup!

"Of homesickness I shall die!
Might I only spy the smoke
Rising from old Stuttgart's flues
When the precious dumplings seethe."

Pity seized me when I heard
This sad story, and I sprang
From my couch and took a seat
By the fireplace and spake:

"Noble poet, tell what chance
Brought thee to this beldam's hut.
Why, oh why, in cruel wise,
Wast thou changed into a dog?"

But the pug exclaimed in joy:
"What! You are no Frenchman then?
But a German, and you've heard
All my hapless monologue?

"Ah, dear countryman, 'twas ill
That old Köllè, Councillor,
When at eve we sat and argued
At the inn o'er pipe and mug,

"Should have harped on the idea
That by travel only might
One attain such culture broad,
As by travel he attained!

"Now, so I might shed the rude
Husk that on my manners lay,
Even as Köllè, and attain
Polish from the world at large,

"To my home I bade farewell,

And in quest of culture came
To the Pyrenees at last,
And Uraka's little hut.

"And a reference I brought
From Justinus Kerner too!
Never did I dream my friend
Stood in league with such a witch!

"Friendly was Uraka's mood,
Till at last with horrid shock,
Lo, I found her friendliness
Had to fiery passion grown.

"Yes, within that withered breast
Lust blazed up in monstrous wise,
And at once this vicious crone
Sought to drag me down to sin.

"Yet I prayed: 'Oh, pardon, ma'am!
Do not fancy I am one
Of those wanton Goethe Bards,—
I belong to Swabia's school.

"'Sweet Morality's our Muse
And the drawers she wears are made
Of the stoutest leather—Oh!
Do not wrong my virtue, pray!

"'Other bards may boast of soul,
Others phantasy—and some
Of their passion—Swabians have
Nothing but their innocence.

"'Nothing else do we possess!
Do not rob me of my pure,
Most religious beggar's cloak,—
Naked else my soul must go!'

"Thus I spoke, whereat the hag
Smiled with hideous irony,
Seized a switch of mistletoe,
Smote me over brow and cheek.

"Chilly spasms seized me then
Just as if a goose's skin
Crept across my limbs—but oh!
This was worse than goose's-skin!

"It was nothing more nor less
Than a dog-pelt! Since that hour,
That accursèd hour, I've lived
Changed into a lumpy pug!"

Luckless wight! his piteous sobs
Now denied him further speech,
And so bitterly he wept
That he half dissolved in tears.

"Hark!" I spoke in pity then,
"Tell me how you might be freed
From this dog-skin. How may I
Give you back to muse and man?"

In despair, disconsolate,
Then he raised his paws in air,
And with sobs and groans at length
Thus his mournful plaint he made:

"Not before the Judgment Day
Shall I shed this horrid form,
If no noble virgin come
To absolve me of the curse.

"None can free me save a maid,
Pure, untouched by any man,
And she must fulfil a pact
Most inexorable—thus:

"Such unspotted maiden must
In Sylvester's holy night
Read the verse of Gustav Pfizer,
Read it and not fall asleep!

"If her chaste eyes do not close
At the reading—then, O bliss!
I shall disenchanted be,
Breathe as man—unpugged at last!"

"In that case, alas," said I,
"Never may I undertake
Your salvation, for you see,
First I am no spotless maid,

"And, still more impossible,
Secondly, I ne'er could read
Any one of Pfizer's poems
And not fall asleep at once."

CANTO XXIII

From this eerie witch-menage
To the valley down we went,
And once more our feet took hold
On the good and solid Earth.

Spectres hence! Hence, gibbering masks!
Shapes of air and fever-dreams!—
Once again, most sensibly
Let us deal with Atta Troll.

In the cavern with his young
Bruin lies in slumber wrapt,
Snoring like an honest soul,
Then he stretches, yawns and wakes.

And young One-Ear crouches down
At his side, his head he rakes
Like a poet seeking rhymes,
And upon his paws he scans.

Close beside the father lie
Atta Troll's belovèd girls,
Pure, four-footed lilies they,
Stretched in dreams upon their backs.

Ah, what tender thoughts must glow
In the budding souls of these
Snow-white virgin bearesses
With their soft and dewy eyes?

And the youngest of them all
Seems most deeply stirred. Her heart,
Smitten by Dan Cupid's shaft,
Quivers with a blissful throe.

Yea, this godling's arrow pierced
Through and through her furry pelt
When she saw him first—Oh, heavens!
'Tis a mortal man she loves!

Man it is—Schnapphahnski named,
Who one day in mad retreat
Passed her as she wandered through
The dim passes of the hills.

Woes of heroes move the fair,
And within our hero's face,
Quite as usual, sorrow lowered,
Pallid care and money-need.

Spent were all his funds of war!
Two-and-twenty silver groats
Taken unto Spain by him
Espartero seized as spoil.

Aye, his very watch was gone!
This in Pampeluna's pawnshop
Lay in bondage. 'Twas a rich
Heirloom all of silver made.

Little thought he as he ran
On his long legs through the woods,
He had won a greater thing
Than a fight—a loving heart!

Yes, she loves him—him the born
Enemy of bears she loves!
Hapless maid! If but your sire
Knew it—oh! what rage were his!

Just like Odoardo old
Who in honest burgess-pride
Stabbed Emilia Galotti—
Even so would Atta Troll

Rather slay his darling lass,
Slay her with his proper paws,
Than that she should ever sink
Even into princely arms!

Yet in this same moment he
Is as softly moved—"no rose
Would he pluck before the storm
Reft it of its petals fair."

Atta Troll in saddest mood
Lies within his rocky cave.
Like Death's warning o'er him creeps
Hunger for infinity.

"Children!" then he sobs, the tears
Burst from out his mournful eyes,—
"Children! soon my earthly days

Shall be ended—we must part.

"Unto me this very noon
Came a dream of import vast,
And my soul drank in the sweet
Sense of early death-to-be.

"Superstitious am I not,
Nor fantastic—ah, and yet
More things lie 'twixt Earth and Heaven
Than philosophy may dream.

"Pondering on the world and fate,
Yawning I had dropped asleep,
And I dreamed that I was lying
Stretched beneath a mighty tree.

"From the branches of this tree
White celestial honey dripped
Straight into my open jaws,
Filling me with wondrous bliss.

"Peering happily aloft
Soon I spied within the leaves
Seven pretty little bears
Gliding up and down the boughs.

"Delicate and dainty things,
All with pelts of rosy hue,
And their heavenly voices rang
Like a melody of flutes!

"As they sang an icy chill
Seized my flesh, although my soul
Like a flame went soaring straight
Gleaming into highest Heaven."

Thus with soft and quivering grunts,
Spake our Atta Troll, then grew
Silent in his wistful grief.
Suddenly his ears he raised,

And in strangest wise they twitched!
Then from up his couch he sprang
Trembling, bellowing with joy:
"Children! do you hear that voice!

"Are not those the dulcet tones
Of your mother? Do I not
My dear Mumma's grumbles know?—
Mumma! Mumma! precious mate!"

Like a madman with these words

From the cave rushed Atta Troll
Swift to his destruction—oh!
To his ruin straight he plunged.

CANTO XXIV

In the Vale of Roncesvalles,
On that very spot where erst
Charlemagne's great nephew fell,
Gasping forth his warrior soul,

Fell and perished Atta Troll,
Fell through ambush, even as he
Whom that Judas of the Knights,
Ganelon of Mainz, betrayed.

Oh! that noblest trait in bears—
Conjugal affection—love—
Formed a pitfall which Uraka
In her evil craft prepared.

For so truly mimicked she
Coal-black Mumma's tender growls,
That poor Atta Troll was lured
From the safety of his lair.

On desire's wings he ran
Through the valley, halting oft
By a rock with tender sniff,
Thinking Mumma there lay hid.

There Lascaro lay, alas,
With his rifle. Swift he shot
Through that gladsome heart a ball,
And a crimson stream welled forth.

Twice or thrice he shakes his head
To and fro, at last he sinks
Groaning, seized with ghastly shudders;—
"Mumma!" is his final sob!

Thus our noble hero fell—
Perished thus. Immortal he
Yet shall live in strains of bards,

Resurrected after death.

He shall rise again in song,
And his wide renown shall stalk
In this blunt trochaic verse
O'er the round and living Earth.

In Valhalla's Hall a shaft
Shall King Ludwig build for him,—
In Bavarian lapidary
Style these words be there inscribed:

ATTA TROLL, REFORMER, PURE,
PIOUS: HUSBAND WARM AND TRUE,
BY THE ZEIT-GEIST LED ASTRAY—
WOOD-ENGENDERED SANS-CULOTTE:

DANCING BADLY: YET IDEALS
BEARING IN HIS SHAGGY BREAST:
OFTTIMES STINKING VERY STRONGLY,
TALENT NONE: BUT CHARACTER.

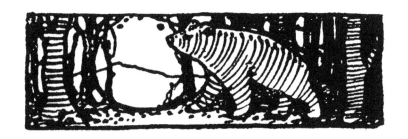

CANTO XXV

Three-and-thirty wrinkled dames,
Wearing on their heads their Basque
Scarlet hoods of ancient style,
Stood beside the village gate.

One of them, like Deborah,
Beat the tambourine and danced
While she sang a hymn in praise
Of the slayer of the bear.

Four strong men in triumph bore
Slaughtered Atta, who erect
In his wicker litter sat
Like some patient at a spa.

To the rear, like relatives
Of the dead, Lascaro came
With Uraka, who abashed,
Nodded to the right and left.

Then the town-clerk at the hall
Spoke as the procession came
To a halt. Of many things
Spoke that dapper little man.

As, for instance, of the rise
Of the navy, of the Press,
Of the sugar-beet debates,
And that hydra, party strife.

All the feats of Louis Philippe
Vaunted he unto the skies,—
Of Lascaro then he spoke
And his great heroic deed.

"Thou Lascaro!" cried the clerk,
As he mopped his streaming brow
With his bright tri-coloured sash—
"Thou Lascaro! thou that hast

"Freed Hispania and France
From that monster Atta Troll,
By both lands shalt be acclaimed the
Pyreneean Lafayette!"

When Lascaro in official
Wise thus heard himself announced
As a hero, then he smiled
In his beard and blushed for joy.

And in stammering syllables
And in broken phrases he
Stuttered forth his gratitude
For the honour shown to him.

Wonder-smitten then stood all
At the unexpected sight,
And in low and timid tones
Thus the ancient women spoke:

"Did you hear Lascaro laugh?
Did you see Lascaro blush?
Did you hear Lascaro speak?
He the witch's perished son!"

On that very day they flayed
Atta Troll. At auction they
Sold his hide. A furrier bid
Just an even hundred francs.

And the furrier decked the skin
Handsomely, and mounted it
All on scarlet. For this work
He demanded twice the cost.

From a third hand Juliet
Then received it. Now it lies
As a rug before her bed
In the city by the Seine.

Oh, how many nights I've stood
Barefoot on the earthly husk
Of my hero great and true,
On the hide of Atta Troll!

Then by sorrow deeply touched
Would I think of Schiller's words:
"That which song would make eternal
First must perish from the Earth."

CANTO XXVI

What of Mumma? Mumma, ah!
Is a woman. Frailty
Is her name! Alas, that women
Should be frail as porcelain!

Now when Fate had parted her
From her great and noble mate,
Did she perish of her woe,
Sinking into hopeless gloom?

Nay, contrarywise, she lived
Merrily as ever—danced
For the public as before,
Eager for their plaudits too.

And at last a splendid place
And support for all her days
Was procured for her in Paris
At the old Jardin-des-Plantes.

There, last Sunday as I strolled
Through that place with Juliet,
Baring Nature's realms to her—
Animal and vegetable,—

Tall giraffes, and cedars brought
Out of Lebanon, the huge
Dromedary, golden pheasants,
And the zebra;—chatting thus,—

We at last stood still and leaned
O'er the rampart of that pit
Where the bears are safely penned—
Heavens! what a sight we saw!

There a huge bear from the wastes
Of Siberia, snowy-white,
Dallied in a love-feast sweet

With a she-bear small and dark.

This was Mumma! This, alas,
Was the mate of Atta Troll!
Well I knew her by the soft
Glances of her dewy eye.

It was she! the daughter dark
Of the Southland! Mumma lives
With a Russian now; she lives
With this savage of the North!

Smirking spake a negro then,
Coming up with stealthy pace:
"Could there be a fairer sight
Than a pair of lovers, say?"

Then I answered him: "Pray, who
Honours me by this address?"
Whereupon he cried amazed:
"Have you quite forgotten me?

"Why I am that Moorish prince
Who beat drums in Freiligrath—
Times were bad—in Germany
I was lonely and forlorn.

"Now as keeper I'm employed
In this garden,—here I find
All the flowers of my native
Tropics,—lions, tigers, too.

"Here I feel content and gay,
Better than at German fairs,
Where each day I beat the drum
And was fed but scantily.

"Late in wedlock was I bound
To a blonde Alsatian cook,
And within her arms I feel
All my native joys again!

"And her feet remind me ever
Of my blessèd elephants,
And her French has quite the ring
Of my sable mother-tongue.

"When she coughs, the rattle fierce
Moves me of that famous drum
Which, bedecked with human skulls,
Drove the snakes and lions far.

"But when moonlight charms her mood,

Like a crocodile she weeps,
Which from out some luke-warm stream
Lifts to gape in cooler air.

"And she cooks me dainty bits.
See, I thrive! I feed again
As upon the Niger I
Fed with gusto African!

"Mark the nicely rounded paunch
I possess! Behold it peeps
From my shirt like some black moon
Stealing forth from whitest clouds."

CANTO XXVII

(To August Varnhagen von Ense)

"Heavens! where, dear Ludoviso,
Did you steal this crazy stuff?"
With these words did Cardinal
D'Este Ariosto greet

When that poet read his work
On Orlando's madness. This
He unto His Eminence
Humbly sought to dedicate.

Yes, Varnhagen, dear old friend,
Yes, I see these very words
Tremble on thy lips, that same
Faint and devastating smile.

Sometimes o'er a book thou laughest,
Then again in earnestness
Thy high forehead wrinkles o'er
As old memories come to thee.

Hark unto the dreams of youth!
Such Chamisso dreamed with me,
And Brentano, Fouqué, too,
In blue nights beneath the moon.

Comes no sound of saintly chimes
From that vanished forest fane,
And no tinkling of the gay
Unforgotten cap-and-bells?

Through the choir of nightingales
Rumbles now the growl of bears,
Low and fierce, and changes then
To the gibbering of ghosts!

Madness in the guise of sense,
Wisdom with a broken spine!

Dying sobs which suddenly
Into hollow laughter pass!

Aye, my friend, such strains arise
From the dream-time that is dead,
Though some modern trills may oft
Caper through the ancient theme.

Spite of waywardness thou'lt find
Here and there a note of pain;—
To thy well-proved mildness now
Do I recommend my song!

'Tis, perchance, the final strain
Of the pure and free Romance:—
In to-day's wild battle-clash,
Miserably it must end.

Other times and other birds!
Other birds and other songs!
What a chattering as of geese
That had saved a capitol!

What a chirping!—sparrows these
Penny tapers in their claws,
Yet have they assumed the ways
Of Jove's eagle with the bolt.

What a cooing! Turtle-doves,
Cloyed with love, now long to hate,
And thenceforth in place of Venus'
They would drag Bellona's car!

What a buzz that shakes the skies!—
These must be the great May-beetles
Of the nation's dawning Spring,
With a Viking fury seized!

Other times and other birds!
Other birds and other songs;—
These, perchance, might yield delight
Were I blest with other ears!

NOTES TO "ATTA TROLL"
BY DR. OSCAR LEVY

PREFACE

THE GOD OF SCHELLING. The German philosopher Schelling (1775-1854) was at first a follower of Spinoza, and had published in his youth a pantheistic philosophy which had made him famous. In later life he began to doubt his former beliefs, and promised to the world another and more Christian explanation of God and the universe. The promised book, however, never appeared.

The gap, thus left by Schelling, has since been filled up by a host of more courageous, if less conscientious, investigators.

"SEA-SURROUNDED SCHLESWIG-HOLSTEIN" OYSTERS. "Schleswig-Holstein Meerumschlungen (sea-surrounded)" was the German Marseillaise after 1846 and again in 1863-64.

ARNOLD RUGE (1802-1880) was the leader of the New Hegelian school, and published certain famous annuals for art and science at Halle. In 1848 he was elected to the Parliament at Frankfort, but was forced to flee to London, where he struck up a fast friendship with Mazzini. In the Revolutionary Committee of London he represented Germany, as Ledru-Rollin represented France and Mazzini Italy.

CHRISTIAN-GERMANIC. One of the favourite phrases and shibboleths of the Romantic School, which may still be heard in the Germany of to-day.

FERDINAND FREILIGRATH (1810-1876). A well-known poet and skilful translator of French and English poets, such as Burns, Byron, Thomas Moore, and Victor Hugo. His own poems betray his dependence upon Hugo. Frederick William IV, King of Prussia, bestowed a pension upon him in 1842. When his friends, however, charged him with having sold himself to the Government, the poet refused the pension. Thereafter he devoted himself more and more to the democratic party and wrote many political poems. In 1848 he went abroad, living in London the greater part of the time. He returned to Germany in 1868, and in 1870 published several patriotic poems which met with great acclaim.

The sudden conversion from international Democracy to Nationalism is easily explained. Modern states have become democratic, and democrats—but they alone—find it easy to feel comfortable and patriotic in such a milieu.

CANTO I

DON CARLOS. After the death of Ferdinand VII of Spain (1833) a lengthy civil war broke out between his younger brother, Don Carlos, and the Queen-widow Christina, who had assumed the regency for her daughter Isabella.

SCHNAPPHAHNSKI. A comic word composed of the German word "schnappen," to snap, and "hahn," cock. It has also been incorporated into French in the form "chenapan." It is applied here to Prince Felix Lichnowski (1814-1848), who left the Prussian Army in 1838 and entered the service of Don Carlos, who appointed him a brigadier-general. After his return from Spain, Lichnowski wrote his "Reminiscences," the publication of which involved him in a duel in which he was badly wounded. The "Reminiscences" are couched in Heine's own style, and their hero is called Schnapphahnski.

JULIET. Juliet is to be understood as referring to Heine's mistress and subsequent wife, Mathilde.

CANTO II

QUEEN MARIA CHRISTINA. She was the wife of Ferdinand VII and assumed the regency after his death. Soon after the king's demise, she married a member of her bodyguard, one Don Ferdinand Muñoz, who was afterwards given the title of Duke of Rianzares. She bore him several children.

PUTANA. Italian for strumpet.

CANTO IV

MASSMANN. A German philologist and one of Heine's favourite butts. He was one of the most enthusiastic advocates of German gymnastics. Athletics was one of the pet ideas of the German patriots; the Government, however, held it in suspicion, inasmuch as the so-called "Turner" (gymnasts) cherished political ambitions. In time, however, the exercise of the muscles cured the revolutionary brain-fag, and the Government was enabled to assume a sort of protectorship over gymnastics. Though enthusiastically carried on to this very day in Germany, the movement no longer has any political significance.

FRESH, PIOUS, GAY, AND FREE. FRISCH, FROMM, FRÖHLICH, FREI—the four F's—formed the motto of the German "Turner."

CANTO V

BATAVIA. Apparently a well-known female ape in Heine's day, trained in theatrical feats of skill.

FREILIGRATH (see above). As a refuge from the crassness of his times, Freiligrath usually chose exotic themes for his poems, frequently African in nature, as, for instance, in his "Löwenritt." The allusion to the mule (in German "camel," which bears the same opprobrious meaning as "ass") gives us reason to believe that Heine's preface must not be taken too seriously and that his opinion of the poet Freiligrath was by no means a high one.

FRIEDRICH LUDWIG GEORG VON RAUMER (1781-1873). A well-known German historian, author of the "History of the Hohenstaufens."

CANTO VIII

TUISKION. The god whom the Germans, according to Tacitus (vide "Germania," cap. II) regard as the original father of their race.

LUDWIG FEUERBACH (1804-1872). An honest thinker, who recognised that there was an unbridgable gulf between philosophy and theology. He left the Hegelian school, which can be so well adapted to the need of theologians, and considered as the only source of religion—the human brain. "The Gods are only the personified wishes of men," he used to say. He brought German philosophy down from the clouds to cookery by declaring: "Der Mensch ist, was er isst" ("Man is what he eats"). He was a believer in what he called "Healthy sensuality," which made him the philosopher of artists in the 'thirties and 'forties of the last century, amongst others of Richard Wagner. The latter, however, afterwards repented, and, by way of Schopenhauer, turned Christian. Feuerbach came from a family that would have been the delight of Sir Francis Galton, author of "Hereditary Genius." Feuerbach's father was a famous jurist, who had five sons, all of whom attained the honour of appearing in the German Encyclopædias. The philosopher was the fourth son. Again: the famous painter Anselm Feuerbach was his nephew, the son of his eldest brother.

BRUNO BAUER (1809-1882). A destructive commentator of the New Testament. He belonged to the school of "higher" criticism which has done so much to "lower" Christianity in the eyes of savants and professors and so little in those of mankind at large. His "Critique of the Evangelistic History of Saint John" (1840) and his "Critique of the Evangelistic Synoptists" (1841-42) had just been published when Heine wrote "Atta Troll."

CANTO IX

MOSES MENDELSOHN (1729-1786). Grandfather of the famous composer. He was a Jewish philosopher and a friend of Lessing's, who, it is supposed, took him as his model for "Nathan the Wise." He freed his German co-religionaries from the oppressive influence of the Talmud.

CANTO X

PROPERTY IS THEFT. A dictum of Prudhon.

CANTO XII

REIGN OF DWARFS. The approaching rule of clever little trades-people, whose turn it will soon be if democracy progresses as at present. Compare Nietzsche's "Zarathustra," Part III, 49, "The Bedwarfing Virtue": "I pass through this people and keep mine eyes open: they have become *smaller*, and ever become *smaller: the reason thereof is their doctrine of happiness and virtue*."

THIS CONCLUSION. "Lo, I kiss, therefore I live"—a witty travesty of Descartes' "Cogito, ergo sum."

CANTO XIV

SO I TOOK TO HUNTING BEARS. Heine considers Atta Troll, the bear bred by the French Revolution, as a much greater and more dangerous foe, and therefore a worthier opponent of his than the sorry German bears—or patriots—with whom he was forced to contend in his native country and who incessantly worried (and still worry) him.

CANTO XV

CAGOTS. The remnant of an ancient tribe, driven out of human society as unclean—Cagot from *Canis gothicus*. The Cagots may still be found in obscure parts of the French Pyrenees; they have their own language and are distinguished by their yellow skins from the peoples of Western Europe. In the Middle Ages they were persecuted as heretics and were excluded from all contact with their neighbours. They were forced to bear a tag upon their clothes so that they might be known as inferiors. Even to-day, despite the fact that they possess the same rights as other Frenchmen, they are considered as somewhat debased and unclean.

CANTO XVIII

THE WILD HUNT which Heine describes in this canto is an old German legend which poets and painters have found to be a fertile source of inspiration. The wild huntsman must ride through the world every night, followed by all evil-doers, and wherever he appears, thither, according to old folk-belief, does misfortune come. Tradition herds all the foes of Christianity among this rout of evil-doers; for this reason does Heine include Goethe—the "great pagan," as the Germans call him—in that crew. There have been other foes of Christianity since, and some very great figures amongst them, so that in time the Wild Huntsman's Company may become quite presentable.

HENGSTENBERG (1802-1869). A fanatical theologian professor at Berlin who made an attack upon Goethe's "Elective Affinities," which then had not yet become a classic, and was thus still liable to the attacks of the "learned."

FRANZ HORN. A contemporary of Heine's of no particular importance, a poet of the Romantic School and a verbose literary historian. He wrote a work in five volumes upon Shakespeare's plays. In this he interprets the poet in a wholly romantic sense and winds up by presenting him as an enthusiastic Christian.

CANTO XIX

ABUNDA—in the Celtic (Breton) folk-lore Dame Abonde and even Dame Habonde. The Celtic element (as, for instance, the legend of King Arthur's Round Table) played a great part in the romantic poetry of Germany, and later in the music dramas of Wagner. Romanticism is therefore represented in Heine's poem by the fairy Abunda, in contradistinction to the Greek and Semitic inspiration—represented by Diana and Herodias. Heine's conception of Herodias as being in love with the Baptist and taking her revenge on him for his Josephian attitude towards her, has, no doubt, influenced later writers on the subject, especially Flaubert and Oscar Wilde, save that these had not the courage (nor perhaps the insight) to regard the hero in question as a "block-head."

CANTO XX

SIX-AND-THIRTY KINGS. At once an allusion to Shakespeare's "A kingdom for a horse!" ("Richard III") and a side-stroke glancing at the various kings and princes of Germany—some thirty-six in Heine's time.

CANTO XXI

HELLISH HERBS. The foul and mouldy herbs and medicines in Uraka's hut represent a collection of remedies for the cure and preservation of decaying feudalism and Christian mediævalism, which, however, no remedy can restore to health. The smell in Uraka's hut is the smell of the "rotting past," that, in spite of all nostrums and artificial revivals, goes on decomposing. The stuffed birds which glare so fixedly and forlorn, and have long bills like human noses, are members of Heine's own race. These stuffed birds are the symbols of Judaism which according to our Hellenistic poet, possesses, as religion, as little life as the Christianity that is based upon it.

CANTO XXII

A SWABIAN BARD. The Swabian school of poetry, of which Uhland was the leader, was the chief representative of German Chauvinism in Heine's day. W. Menzel, the critic who denounced "Young Germany" to the Government, belonged to this school. Börne answered him in his "Menzel der Franzosenfresser" ("The Gallophobe"), and Heine mocked at him in his paper "The Denunciator." Gustav Pfizer (who had provoked Heine) and Karl Meyer were members of the Swabian school, and prided themselves particularly upon their morality and religiosity, for which reason they set themselves in antagonism to the "heathen" Goethe. Goethe, on his part, estimated this school as little as did Heine. In a letter to Zelter dated October 5, 1831, Goethe writes thus of Pfizer: "...I read a poem lately by Gustav Pfizer ... the poet appears to have real talent and is evidently a very good man. But as I read I was oppressed by a certain poverty of spirit in the piece and put the little book away at once, for with the advance of the cholera it is well to shield oneself against all debilitating influences. The work is dedicated to Uhland, and one might well doubt if anything exciting, thorough, or humanly compelling could be produced from those regions in which he is master. I will therefore not rail at the work, but simply leave it alone. *It is really marvellous how these little men are able to throw their goody-religious-poetic beggar's cloak so cleverly about their shoulders that, whenever an elbow happens to stick out, one is tempted to consider this as a deliberate poetic intention.*"

METZEL-SOUP. A Swabian soup of the country districts, glorified in the poetry of Uhland. It is usually prepared from the "insides" of pigs.

CHRISTOPHER FRIEDRICH K. VON KÖLLE (1781-1848). A Privy Councillor of the Legation of Würtemberg—composer of many poems and political pamphlets.

JUSTINUS KERNER (1786-1862) was also a poet of the Swabian school. He believed in spirits, and made many observations and experiments in his house at Weinsburg in order to obtain some knowledge of the supernatural world. Thousands of those who believed, or wished to believe, came to his "séances." He worked in conjunction with a celebrated medium of his time, and later published a very successful book about this lady. Heine, no doubt, had this medium in mind when he mentioned Kerner.

CANTO XXIII

BALDOMERO ESPARTERO (1792-1879). A celebrated Spanish general who fought against Don Carlos on the side of Maria Christina. He was later given the title of Duke of Vittoria.

EMILIA GALOTTI. This refers to the heroine of Lessing's drama of the same name, in which old Odoardo Galotti slays his daughter in order to protect her from dishonour. The theme is derived from the story of Virginia and Tarquin.

"NO ROSE WOULD HE PLUCK, ETC." Lessing's drama closes thus: "*Odoardo*: 'God! what have I done!' *Emilia*: 'Thou hast merely plucked a rose ere the storm reft it of its petals.'"

CANTO XXIV

GANELON OF MAINZ was the stepfather of Roland, against whom he bore a grudge. He contrived to bring about his destruction by betraying him to the Saracens, who over-powered and killed him in the Valley of Roncesvalles, as related in the well-known "Chanson de Roland."

VALHALLA'S HALL. King Ludwig I of Bavaria ordered a Greek temple to be built on the banks of the Danube near Regensburg, to which he gave the name of Valhalla. In this the busts of all great Germans are placed—as, for instance, with great ceremony, that of Bismarck some years ago, and recently that of Wagner. Atta Troll's epitaph is a satirical imitation of the poetic effusions of Ludwig I, who considered himself a poet but was nothing more than an affected versifier. His mania for compression and for participial forms (not to be tolerated in German) more than once drew the arrows of Heine's wit. The last line: "Talent none, but character," has become a familiar phrase in Germany.

CANTO XXV

PYRENEEAN LAFAYETTE. Lafayette fought for the Revolution in France as well as in America.

"THAT WHICH SONG WOULD MAKE ETERNAL," &c. A quotation in a semi-satiric vein from Schiller's "The Gods of Greece."

CANTO XXVI

DROVE THE SNAKES AND LIONS FAR. A burlesque quotation from Freiligrath's poem "Der Löwenritt," from which also the reference later on to the crocodile is taken.

CANTO XXVII

VARNHAGEN VON ENSE (1785-1858). After abandoning his career as a diplomat, von Ense married the celebrated Rahel. He lived in Berlin, where the salon of his wife became the meeting-ground for artists and writers. In his youth he associated closely with the romantics—de la Motte Fouqué, Chamisso, and Clemens Brentano, the brother of Bettina von Arnim. Though imitating the heavy and cautious style of the later Goethe he was a good writer, and his biographies of celebrated men belong to the best in German literature. He endeavoured, but without success, to win over the all-powerful Austrian Minister Metternich to the cause of "Young Germany."

OTHER TIMES AND OTHER BIRDS! These words refer to the new generation of poets—Georg Herwegh, Friedrich Freiligrath, Dingelstedt, Hoffmann von Fallersleben, and Anastasius Grün—who came upon the scene about 1840, cherished mechanic-democratic ideals and brought about the Revolution of 1848. Heine, by nature an aristocratic poet, who instinctively dreaded the competition of "noble bears," saw all his loftiest principles trodden into the mire by these Utopian hotheads and the crew of politicians that came storming after them. This doctrinaire and numerical interpretation of the rights of man—for which rights in their proper application the poet himself had fought so valiantly—caused him great unhappiness. He now saw his fairest concepts (as is made clear in his own introduction) distorted as in some crooked mirror, and so, filled with anger, grief and disgust, he conceived and wrote his lyrico-satiric masterpiece, "Atta Troll." The poem has been misunderstood to this very day, for the mechanics and theorists have practically won. *The day it is understood, their reign will be over.*

Lector House believes that a society develops through a two-fold approach of continuous learning and adaptation, which is derived from the study of classic literary works spread across the historic timeline of literature records. Therefore, we aim at reviving, repairing and redeveloping all those inaccessible or damaged but historically as well as culturally important literature across subjects so that the future generations may have an opportunity to study and learn from past works to embark upon a journey of creating a better future.

This book is a result of an effort made by Lector House towards making a contribution to the preservation and repair of original ancient works which might hold historical significance to the approach of continuous learning across subjects.

HAPPY READING & LEARNING!

LECTOR HOUSE LLP
E-MAIL: lectorpublishing@gmail.com

9 789353 448554

CPSIA information can be obtained
at www.ICGtesting.com
Printed in the USA
LVHW100103210323
742068LV00030B/1073